Kristin and Danny are two people we car[...] sometimes even laugh until you cry with [...] no exception! Their stories will make you [...] want to put it down.

Adam and Danielle Busby, stars of the
hit reality show *OutDaughtered*

Kristin and Danny share their story with humor and much wisdom. *The Road to Love and Laughter* will leave you inspired and feeling like you're not alone. It's so refreshing to see a real behind-the-scenes look at someone's life and remember that the beauty of life is the full journey.

Jeremy and Audrey Roloff, *New York Times* bestselling authors

Kristin and Danny have a unique way of blending humor and wisdom into a single conversation. Their words, stories, and fun approach to life and love will leave you feeling encouraged and inspired to live each moment—even the hard and imperfect ones—to the fullest. Prepare to simultaneously nod your head in agreement and chuckle to yourself as you thumb through these pages. This book is a gift, the words inside are a treasure, and the hearts behind every letter are made of gold.

Jordan Lee Dooley, national bestselling author

The Road to Love and Laughter is one of those books that just makes you feel good. It's written from the heart with a great deal of honesty. I have the good fortune of knowing Kristin and Danny personally, and I was pleasantly surprised at what I was able to learn about them through these pages. Their challenges, both good and bad, inspire me as a friend, and now, as authors, they can inspire legions of people they may never meet face-to-face! I highly recommend *The Road to Love and Laughter* to anyone who thinks their dreams can't or won't happen. Danny and Kristin have proved that they can.

Butch Hartman, Hollywood entertainment
executive, creator of *The Fairly OddParents*

We're all looking for love. Once we find it, it sometimes turns out to be challenging and perplexing. Kristin and Danny have a gift for helping you solve the riddle of love. You'll be laughing and relaxing as you learn to be loved and give love like never before. This book will remind you why you chose your spouse and guide you toward the marriage you dreamed of when you first said "I do."

John S. Dickerson, lead pastor of Connection
Pointe Christian Church, Brownsburg, Indiana

Had you told me that a book about marriage—one built on biblical principles and time-tested relationship wisdom—would make me laugh out loud, I would not have believed you. (I own at least twenty books about marriage, and not once have I even chuckled.) But in *The Road to Love and Laughter*, Kristin and Danny Adams prove (in case there was any doubt) that they are more than just a couple of pretty faces who know how to lip sync. Whether you're married or hoping to be, this book will equip you to grow in (and fight for) your love, trust God to redeem and shape you, and have a whole lot of fun as you do. Buy a copy for yourself and then wrap one up with every wedding gift you give from now on.

Jodie Berndt, bestselling author of the
Praying the Scriptures book series

You will come away changed after reading *The Road to Love and Laughter*! It felt like sitting down with our sweet friends and mentors, being encouraged, enriched, and propelled to love each other better. Kristin and Danny exude God's joy and grace, and they lead with humility. This is a must-read!

Jefferson and Alyssa Bethke, *New York Times* bestselling
authors of *Love That Lasts, To Hell with the Hustle,* and *Satisfied*

Kristin and Danny have written a book on such an important subject in a way that only the two of them could. With humor, insight, empathy, and wisdom, they help us know that marriage is not for the faint of heart. Yet it can be so rewarding when two imperfect people learn to communicate in healthy ways and choose to give grace before it's deserved. By sharing their own failures, struggles, and setbacks, they give us the encouragement and hope we need to build strong marriages!

Aaron Brockett, lead pastor of Traders Point
Christian Church, Indianapolis, Indiana

The ROAD to LOVE and *Laughter*

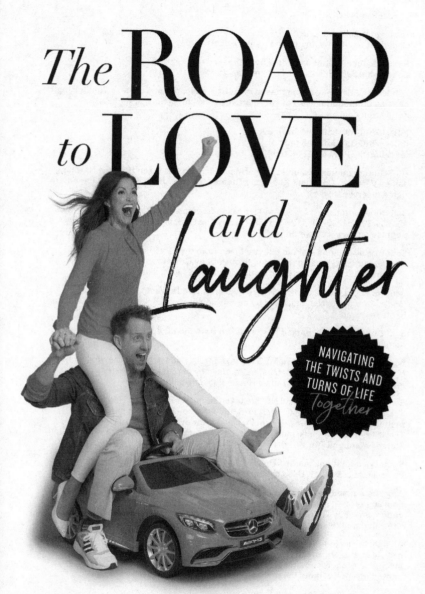

The ROAD to LOVE and *Laughter*

NAVIGATING THE TWISTS AND TURNS OF LIFE *Together*

KRISTIN AND DANNY ADAMS

ZONDERVAN BOOKS

ZONDERVAN BOOKS

The Road to Love and Laughter
Copyright © 2021 by Kristin and Danny Adams

Requests for information should be addressed to:
Zondervan, 3900 Sparks Dr. SE, Grand Rapids, Michigan 49546

Zondervan titles may be purchased in bulk for educational, business, fundraising, or sales promotional use. For information, please email SpecialMarkets@ Zondervan.com.

ISBN 978-0-310-36054-4 (softcover)
ISBN 978-0-310-36056-8 (audio)
ISBN 978-0-310-36055-1 (ebook)

Published in association with Punchline Agency LLC.

Photos from the authors unless otherwise noted.

Cover design and photo: Micah Kandros
Interior design: Denise Froehlich

Printed in the United States of America

21 22 23 24 /LSC/ 10 9 8 7 6 5 4 3 2 1

For our daughter, Harper, and our son, Holt.
You are our greatest gifts. We pray that you will live loudly,
love radically, and laugh uncontrollably for the rest of your
lives. Keep God first and remember that nothing you do
can make Him love you more, and nothing you do can
make Him love you less. You are His and He is yours.

Harper (9 yrs.), Holt (6 yrs.)

CONTENTS

FOREWORD

S arah and I consider Kristin and Danny good friends, and we love their two children, Holt and Harper.

They have spent a lot of time in our home, making us laugh.

One memorable story they told us about comes from a Greek friend of theirs. When she'd engage in discussions that turned heated and the other person stopped listening to her, she'd end the conversation by declaring in her strong accent, "Life gonna show you."

Kristin and Danny gifted us with that slogan, which they had framed. It hangs on our wall: "Life gonna show you." Kristin's rendition of this lady echos in my ears each time I read it, and I smile.

That slogan represents much of this book. Life has shown Danny and Kristin a thing or two. Maybe one thing most of all: Proverbs 17:22 (ESV), "A joyful heart is good medicine." This is their life message.

You will learn that they spent time in Hollywood. They have observed the marriages of the rich and famous. The secret is out. No one has a perfect marriage. For Danny and Kristin, the key and call are to be real, not unreal, and to fight against projecting happy smiles on social media, to be envied by others, yet living unhappily off camera.

They have worked at the art and science of bringing joy to their hearts and marriage through laughter.

Yes, they have comedic ability. But this isn't about jokes per se. It's more about joy, and they know the difference. They believe they are called to remind the rest of us that we need a good dose of medicine, and a joyful heart is the prescription.

Their prayer is that we would hear them about the healing that comes from a good chuckle.

This really is a choice and discipline, not about being a born jokester. They have learned, and still are learning, to navigate conflict by bringing the discipline of laughter into the relationship—at the right time.

Like the rest of us, they go down in sadness when a marital misunderstanding arises. Still, they come back up by not only resolving the misunderstanding but also seeking to be joyful again. They do not do this every time. No one does. But they have learned to do it more often than most, and from them, we can learn a thing or two. Finding the joy and humor can be a serious matter.

They have accepted that there will be heated fellowship between two believers in Christ. When such tension arises, they know how to rebound successfully from the normal misunderstandings between a husband and wife. They have the know-how when it comes to navigating these heated moments with a little knowledge, skill, and fortitude.

Welcome to the road to love and laughter.

Danny and Kristin "gonna show you."

EMERSON EGGERICHS, PhD
Author of *Love and Respect*

INTRODUCTION

Kristin: Hey, guys! I'm Kristin . . .

Danny: and I'm Danny . . .

K & D: Wassup!

Danny: If you've seen one of our videos, you know this has been our greeting in every one of them. You also may already know the tagline we strive to live out, our mantra that *laughter is the best medicine.*

Kristin: Unless, of course, you need actual medicine.

Danny: Yeah, then you should take that too.

Kristin: More specifically, beyond the millions who have seen our lip sync videos, many have also seen our family travel vlogs, where we're laughing together and having a good time on road trips.

Danny: From the outside looking in, our lives may appear as just one big slaphappy party, 24-7.

Kristin: Yes. But the truth is that anyone can look like they have it all together in a three-minute video clip.

Danny: Right, when in fact there are twenty-three hours and fifty-seven minutes left in the day where we both approach life very differently.

Kristin: And those differences can eventually lead to conflict. And unresolved conflict, when compounded over time—like, for example, twelve years of marriage—can make you want to . . .

Danny: drive off a cliff?

Kristin: Wow, okay. I was going to say something along the lines of "look for the nearest exit ramp," but that's another way to take things. Then again, there have definitely been moments when we've wanted to call it quits. I mean, once upon a time, we were a hot mess.

Danny: Now we're just a mess.

Kristin: I mean, at least we dropped the "hot." Progress over perfection—isn't that what all the internet gurus say? So we'll be the first to admit that we don't have this marriage thing completely nailed just yet.

Danny: We're not marriage experts.

Kristin: But there is one thing we know for sure. No marriage is free of conflict.

Danny: Because every marriage is made up of two flawed people.

Kristin: Exactly. And in our case, one slightly flawed girl and one majorly flawed guy, you know, but the ratio isn't really the point here.

Danny: Then what is the point?

Kristin: The point is that we can't get rid of conflict altogether. It's part of our sin DNA that's always going to be there to some degree. But what we can do is shorten the distance between the offense and the reconciliation. So for us, what used to take three days of silent treatment to get over a fight, now only takes us, like . . .

Danny: two and a half days.

Kristin: Yes!

Danny: Baby steps.

Kristin: It's only taken us twelve years of marriage to shave off half a day! Just think of where we'll be in another twelve years. At some point, we may even be able to get through our morning coffee without conflict.

Danny: I mean, with God, *all* things are possible.

Kristin: Amen. Testify.

Danny: Throughout the tough times and difficulties and all the twists and turns of marriage, we have to remind ourselves that we're in this together. We are on the same team.

Kristin: Absolutely. As we look in the rearview mirror of our little road trip metaphor here,

God has always brought good out of any wrong turns we've made. There have been several potholes and some major roadblocks for sure, but things have always gotten better because we chose to trust God and weather the storms *together*.

Danny: And we're still mostly intact! That mindset—that we are truly better together—is what we're betting will get us through the next twelve years of marriage.

Kristin: And the next. So our hope with this book is to convince you that you can get through anything with the right amount of love and laughter and that God will use our story, both individually and as a couple, to encourage you and others to stay in the fight. Or at least in the car. There will be huge wins and losses in life and in marriage, but the key to having joy throughout the journey is keeping your heart light and free of the stuff that tries to weigh it down.

Danny: That's the hope. We're going to share our tips and tricks for "staying in the car" together. And some of our most personal stories, right?

Kristin: Yes. And how to keep the laughter flowing in the midst of work, ministry, raising kids, and all the things . . .

Danny: and how we've learned to celebrate our differences and believe the best in each other.

Kristin: But just a little disclaimer before you start reading this book. If you don't get anything out of it, remember, you're the one who bought a marriage book from an internet couple.

Danny: Though if it does end up changing your life, we want the credit.

Kristin: Well, shouldn't God get the credit?

Danny: Okay, ninety percent our credit, ten percent God.

Kristin: Ooh, nice. Like a glory tithe.

Danny: Exactly.

Kristin: So, any ideas on how we should officially start this book?

Danny: How about a knock-knock joke?

Kristin: Um, I was thinking something more along the lines of, "Wherever you're at on your road together, we invite you to join us on a trip through the many unexpected experiences of our first twelve years of marriage and what they taught us about keeping our tanks filled to enjoy far more of the journey than we probably would have otherwise."

Danny: Okay . . . I guess that works too.

Enjoying the journey together, Martha's Vineyard, 2014.

CHAPTER 1

OUR HOLLYWOOD SETUP

Kristin: In some ways, I'm glad our story began before social media was a thing.

Danny: Back when the only way to really get to know someone was face-to-face.

Kristin: Right. Do you remember the first time we met?

Danny: Oh, our rookie year, huh?

Kristin: FYI, everything Danny contributes to this book is going to be by way of a sports analogy, just so you know.

Danny: Of course. We met during a time in my life when my team had just come off of a losing season. Then I walked into the locker room, and there you were. The newly acquired free agent.

Kristin: Oh my, just stop.

Danny: Actually, I remember the first time we met very well. You, on the other hand . . .

Kristin: Hey, I remember the party where we met, just not meeting you at that party.

Danny: Yeah, apparently it was only life-changing for one of us. I'm still getting over that one.

Kristin: I don't know if this is a gender stereotype reversal, but you're typically the one with the detailed memory. Crazy details sometimes. Down to the minute things about events that happened decades ago. Me? I can't even remember what I had for breakfast.

Danny: The first time we met, I had been living in Los Angeles for about a year, and you walked into a little house party of some friends of mine who were living in Burbank at the time.

Kristin: Wow, Burbank? See, I definitely don't remember that.

Danny: Yeah, they had invited some people over to hang out and have some chili, and then in walks this new girl that no one knew. So, yeah, my ears may have perked up a bit. I remember you were wearing blue jeans and a red turtleneck.

Kristin: Seriously? You remember that?

Danny: And it was 9:17 p.m., 72 degrees, with partly cloudy skies and a twenty percent chance of rain.

Kristin: Wow, that's a wee bit freaky. Honestly, your memory is one of the things I most love and hate about you. Because you remember things that I'm grateful you remember, like details from one of our trips or family vacations. But then you go and remember things that I wish you would forget, like specifics about mean things I've said to you over the years or a look I gave when you were, you know, making another bonehead move while driving.

Danny: It's details. It's all about details. And I vividly remember more about things that are relational. Relationships and people. History and science facts? Not so much.

Kristin: (laughs) In this instance, I do appreciate that you remember these details, because now I know I was wearing blue jeans and a red turtleneck at a party in Burbank, California, and that there was chili being served on the day we met. Thank you very much.

Danny: There you go. So you walked in, and everyone was introducing themselves to you, and I kinda stood back and waited for my moment. I didn't want to seem overanxious, like "Hey! Hey! I'm Danny! What's your name? You're new, aren't you?" I was like, I'm gonna play this cool. Gonna sit back, talk to other girls, like maybe you would notice that all the other girls are cool with me. I wasn't just lurking in the corner, chewing my nails and staring at you all weird and creepy.

Kristin: I sure hope not. In any case, I was totally oblivious.

Danny: I had this whole fantasy of how it'd play out in my mind. Me walking over, introducing myself, and you being like, "Oh my goodness, the man of my dreams." But in reality, I walked over after the dust cleared from the stampede of guys who introduced themselves to you—

Kristin: See, now, I don't remember a stampede of guys.

Danny: Oh, a stampede happened. The dust barely cleared, but I wasn't waiting for a tumbleweed. I came in and was like, "I'll be your Huckleberry."

Kristin: (courtesy laugh)

Danny: No, I said, "Hey, I'm Danny. Can I get you something to drink?" You said a Jack and Coke, and then I looked down at my Zima and thought, "Okay. Maybe this isn't a match."

Kristin: Oh no, did I really request a Jack and Coke?

Danny: No, actually, you asked for red wine.

Kristin: Okay, phew!

Danny: Your Jack and Coke phase didn't start until about a year later.

Kristin: Yeah, we'll get to that. Red wine, though—that's a solid choice. Way fewer red flags attached to that drink order.

Danny: So I brought you a glass of wine and made some small talk. I asked what brought you to LA, and you mentioned *American Idol.*

Kristin: I had just finished competing on season one, and at that time, I think we were on the road for season two. They'd hired me to cohost the audition episodes with Ryan Seacrest.

Danny: And you were in town filming the LA auditions.

Kristin: So I was already "the girl who fell down on season one."

Danny: Yeah, but at that point, I didn't know about your epic fall.

Kristin: Wait, are you telling me you weren't an avid *American Idol* watcher?

Danny: Well, not an avid one, but I did watch the show a bit. I remember going to the taping of the season-one top-three performance. A friend of mine, who is good friends with Seacrest, invited me to go.

Kristin: We should stop right here and talk about how when you live in LA, whether you're in the entertainment industry or not, if you live there for any length of time, you inevitably find yourself connected to people in the industry.

Danny: Absolutely.

Kristin: Especially when you're young and live in the Valley and all that jazz.

Danny: Yeah, like, we're all connected to Kevin Bacon somehow.

Kristin: Yes! We're all six degrees of separation from Kevin Bacon. Six degrees of separ-Bacon!

Danny: The Baconator.

Kristin: So you went to one of the final shows during season one, but I had already been voted off at that point.

Danny: Right. Kelly Clarkson ended up winning that season, so I have to admit, it was pretty cool to see her perform. But back to the house party—after some small talk, that was pretty much it. The party ended, a group of us walked out together, and it was simply an "Alright, see ya around" kind of thing.

Kristin: Which may be why I don't remember it.

Danny: Then, the second time I saw you, I found out that you were in a serious relationship.

Kristin: Yes, my college sweetheart situation.

Danny: You had gone back to Dallas for a few months, only to return shortly thereafter for more obligations with *Idol*. Then you showed up at a Super Bowl party that another friend of ours was having at his place. I remember it was the Oakland Raiders versus the Tampa Bay Buccaneers, Super Bowl 37.

Kristin: Okay, Freaky Memory Man strikes again! So our first two meetings were at house parties.

Danny: Yes, and the second time you brought your boyfriend with you. And I was like, "Oh, she mentioned nothing about this boyfriend the first time around. What is goin' on?" I mean, obviously I thought you were cute, but once I realized you had a boyfriend, I was like, "Ah, rats! Boyfriend."

Kristin: Did you really say, "Rats!" in your head?

Danny: I did. I was like, "Rats! Man, oh man."

Kristin: Then did you take your wooden baseball bat and go hit some balls outside?

Danny: I did. And then I saw my friend had some cold meat hanging from a tree, so I turned on my cassette tape of the *Rocky* theme song, punched the meat for a while, and then came back to the party dripping with sweat.

Kristin: And smelling of raw meat.

Danny: Delicious.

Kristin: And then you came over and met my boyfriend.

Danny: Well, I walked up to you because I had met you once before and, of course, you had made an impression on me, you know, with your stunning beauty and whatnot.

Kristin: Aw, thanks.

Danny: I mean, settle down, I wasn't writing your name on my wall or anything. But I did want to meet this guy because he seemed pretty cool.

Kristin: Which is totally you, babe. You want to meet *everybody* in the room.

Danny: It's true. So we started talking, and I ended up connecting with him because we were both former college athletes. Honestly, I probably had more in common with him than anyone in the room because most of the other guys were—

Kristin: young Hollywood types.

Danny: Yeah. Not that I didn't have things in common with them, but the three of us ended up talking and laughing, and it was fun getting to know both of you.

Kristin: Ironically, when we left the party that day, my boyfriend said, "Man, that Danny guy is really cool. You should stay friends with him when you move out here."

Danny: Mwahahaha . . . little did he know.

Kristin: Haha. For the record, you and I didn't feel anything romantic toward each other at that point. I was in a committed relationship and was completely focused on *American Idol*, hosting, and trying to get relocated to LA.

Danny: Right, and I had my head down pursuing my career too. I was dating, but not anything serious. Plus, I respected the fact that you were in a relationship, so I didn't have—

Kristin: ulterior motives.

Danny: No, not at all. I thought you were a pretty girl, but you know . . .

Kristin: We're a dime a dozen, just say it.

Danny: Well, there are pretty girls all day long in LA. But when your boyfriend suggested, "Hey, maybe Danny can be someone you can go to," I took that seriously, kind of like . . .

Kristin: a big brother.

Danny: I'm a few years older than you, and I had seen people come out to LA and get chewed up by the industry. Especially if they were a little naive. It's helpful to have friends to connect with and get some direction. And so I did take a big brother role. I remember from that point over the course of the next month or so, you came to LA a couple of times from Dallas, and I picked you up from the airport.

Kristin: Which I came to learn is a big deal in LA—picking someone up from the airport.

Danny: It is. Traffic is a beast, so a trip to and from the airport or helping someone move are two of the biggest acts of service you can do for anyone.

Kristin: And you helped me move into my first apartment in LA, so I'm two for two.

Danny: Well, I owned a pickup truck at the time, so everyone and their grandma was asking me for help.

Kristin: And your little Enneagram-two self just couldn't say no.

Early dating years: celebrating Danny's birthday at a bowling center in Los Angeles, 2005.

Danny: Pretty much. I genuinely just wanted to look out for you, and I was glad to be someone you could trust. I wasn't necessarily thinking it would lead to something romantic, but I mean, hey, if it did, that would definitely be a bonus.

Kristin: Meeting you early on was huge because it brought me a sense of peace. I mean, even though I was ambitious and fearless, I was still just twenty-one years old and overwhelmed, so it did feel good to know— and I've always thought this about you—that you're a really good guy. You know? And maybe some people think, "Aw, you don't want to be the good guy." Like, I friend-zoned you right out of the gate. But, honestly, goodness and decency are lost traits these days. And you've always had both. I've always felt safe with you.

Danny: Real talk. Thanks, babe.

Kristin: Now, hold on, I wasn't rushing home to write your name on my wall yet either. It took me another three years to realize you were "the one." But God knew what He was doing. And we both had some serious growing up to do.

Danny: Totally. Maybe your *American Idol* story should come next.

Kristin: You mean the one where I fell down on national television in front of millions of people?

Danny: Yeah, that one.

Kristin: I'm just now getting over the embarrassment of it all. What are you trying to do? Send me back to therapy?

Danny: No, of course not! I just really wanna laugh.

CHAPTER 2

LEARNING TO ACT "AS IF . . ."

Kristin

Danny and I met during one of the most exciting times of my life. I had just finished competing on the first season of this new show called *American Idol* as a top thirty finalist. And now I was in the middle of cohosting season two with Ryan Seacrest. In the months ahead, I would relocate from my hometown of Plano, Texas, to the bright lights of Hollywood, for what would prove to be an experience that would forever change the course of my life.

It's strange now to recount the details of this story; I almost feel like I'm writing about someone else's life, partly because the whole *American Idol* thing was surreal to begin with and partly because I'm a completely different person than I was at the time of filming the show. Giving your heart to Jesus will do that to you. Making a ton of mistakes, both personally and professionally, will do that to you too, I guess. Now, nearly eighteen years removed, I look back at the girl I once was and who I am today, and I thank God for His mercy, grace, and transformative power. It will forever be a mystery to me how He takes the highs and lows of our life, the wins and losses and everything in between, and uses it all for our good and for His glory.

But the truth is, though I placed highly and did well on that first season, I almost didn't show up to the first round of auditions in Dallas. For one, singing was something I'd always enjoyed, but only as a hobby. My singing was mostly reserved for times when I was alone, like in the car or the shower. And, news flash, *everyone* sounds good in the shower. Also, just getting myself to the audition was a lot of work. It was the spring of 2002, and I was finishing up my junior year at Texas Christian University. I was in the midst of studying for my final exams and simultaneously preparing to compete in the Miss Texas pageant that summer. If you don't know about Texas beauty pageants, let me digress for a moment here.

I didn't grow up competing in pageants, but it's basically an unwritten rule in Texas that all young women of a certain type have to compete in at least one pageant or they'll kick you out of the state. I didn't necessarily consider myself the type, so competing was never on my radar until I met a friend in college who was runner-up in the Miss America competition earlier that year. She nearly paid for law school with her scholarship award money. And that, my friends, was when I realized I *was* the type. That was all the incentive I needed to enter myself into the next nearest local pageant competition, which just so happened to be down the road from my university in the small town of Burleson, Texas.

It's a pretty big state, but you're never more than a few miles away from a pageant in Texas.

I assumed you had to be from the town in which you competed, but that's apparently not the case. You can literally travel all over the great state of Texas competing in local pageants until you win a city title before heading to the state competition. So that's exactly what I had planned on doing, but surprisingly, I won the Burleson pageant! I had heard stories of how hard it was to break into the pageant system and thought I was probably going to have to compete several times before winning anything. Yes, "the system" has its own local lore and gossip groupies. But then *bam!* There I was, standing on a stage with a new fancy title and a big ole bouquet of flowers in my hands. Also imagine a sparkly crown on my head and a pageant representative singing, "There she is, Miss Burleson," proudly into a microphone. The tears are *real*, y'all.

So, needless to say, that particular week when *Idol* came to town, I was juggling a lot. And not for the talent portion, if you

Kristin with her parents after being crowned Miss Burleson 2002.

know what I mean. I had a college final scheduled during the time the auditions were in town, but after one of my professors graciously agreed to move the exam to another day, I decided to make the thirty-minute drive across town over to the Wyndham Anatole Hotel in Dallas for what I thought would be a quick in-and-out audition for this new singing-competition-reality-show-thingy. But when I pulled up only to witness thousands of other hopefuls standing in a seemingly never-ending line that wrapped multiple times around the building, I began to second-guess myself.

Remember, this was back in the spring of 2002, the cusp of reality television, before *American Idol* had ever hit the airwaves. I didn't know if ten or ten thousand people were going to show up to the audition. And I'm glad I didn't know, because had I known, I wonder if I still would've shown up, knowing how crazy difficult it would be even to have the chance to audition. I truly applaud the hundreds of thousands of people who tried out in the subsequent seasons, knowing that their chances of making it through were slim to none.

That being said, I was raised to believe I could do anything I put my mind to (thank you, Mom and Dad), regardless of the odds. Even if I had little to no experience in whatever the thing was, I fully believed I could do it, or that I could just figure it out on the fly. This mindset served me well, as almost every audition or entertainment-industry job I booked without the résumé or experience to back it up happened because I showed up acting as if I already had the job.

So I mustered up some Texas-sized courage and took my place in the sea of other singers waiting for their chance to sing in front of the judges. As I waited in line, I found myself in conversation with some of the other contestants, including Kelly Clarkson! But she wasn't *the* Kelly Clarkson yet. She was just, you know, basic Kelly Clarkson at this point, before "Miss Independent" and "Since U Been Gone" and "Stronger" and the countless other hits we all know and love. Turns out that she is from Burleson, Texas, and ended up recognizing me from all my pageant duties around town. Y'all, I wasn't even wearing my pageant sash or crown or anything, and she recognized me! This is the first time anyone had ever recognized me as Miss Burleson, which goes to show how big of a deal pageants can be in small-town America. My cutting the ribbon at the local Walmart and riding a steer in the Burleson parade were not in vain because, y'all, Kelly Clarkson just recognized me! Unfortunately, I've lost touch with her over the years, but I can tell you that back then, and in the early years after her newfound fame, this is exactly how she was—down-to-earth and kind as can be.

Now, on *Idol*, there are several rounds contestants go through to determine whether they make it through to sing in front of the official judges. I later learned that the producers put the best singers through (to find a legitimate winner), the worst singers through (because that makes great television), and if they are on the fence, then your "story" may get you through. I'm fairly confident that I fell into that third category. I may not have Kelly Clarkson pipes, but I don't sound like a wounded cat either. Being somewhere in the middle, my advantage *had* to be my story. Of course, there was the "pageant girl" thing, but I also happened to be a former Dallas Cowboys Cheerleader.

Okay, maybe I should have led with this, but you probably have the mental image already—white cowboy boots, hot pants, the whole shebang. Oh, and this was another job I got through the law of "acting as if." Seriously. Outside of one year on my junior high drill team, I had never officially cheered a day in my life before making the team. Not only did I make it, but I was then placed on their elite "show group" squad made up of the twelve best dancers on the team who, in addition to cheering at the Cowboys games, traveled around the world entertaining US troops on USO tours. But don't be fooled. I didn't make the squad because I'm some sort of an incredible dancer or cheerleader. I was still a part of all the dance routines, but I was typically placed in the back row toward either the far right or left of the stage. And, depending on the venue, there was often a large pole, curtain, or podium obstructing my view of the audience. Now, if I couldn't see the crowd very well, it's likely they couldn't see me either. I started to realize that this particular placement probably wasn't accidental. So, no, I didn't make it onto the team because of my extraordinary dance skills. I made it onto the team because I just so happened to audition in a year when they needed a singer to entertain crowds between dance numbers. Timing really is everything.

Like my *Idol* audition, I almost didn't show up to the DCC audition either, because when I pulled up to Texas Stadium and saw a line of what seemed like a thousand blond bombshells with their hair in Velcro rollers and impeccable makeup, I looked in the mirror at my flat, unteased hair, glanced down at the audition outfit I was wearing—a borrowed leotard and tights from a dance major who lived down the hall in my freshman dorm at TCU—and figured it would probably be best for me turn around and head back to campus. But after a quick phone call and pep talk from my mom, who encouraged me to "get in there, do your best, and show 'em what you've got," I reluctantly changed my mind. And I'm so glad I did. We miss 100 percent of the shots we never take. And sometimes, even when you feel underqualified or not good enough, if you just "act as if" you've already got the job, well, sometimes you even fool yourself.

To my surprise, I continued to make it through each round of the auditions, which lasted well over a week. We were tested on our dance ability, how well we can pick up dance choreography, how well we could perform in a kick line (which I turned out to be pretty good at thanks to several years of martial arts training when I was younger), and our interview skills. And the final round was the talent portion. For this round, where nearly every girl chooses to perform an original dance routine, I opted to sing and play a song on my guitar. I played "Cowboy Take Me Away" by the Dixie Chicks, but changed the lyric to "Cowboys take me away." See what I did there? #imsoclever

Kristin's official headshot for the Dallas Cowboys Cheerleaders, 2000–2001 season.

However, when the judges' panel called my number to come up and perform, I couldn't quickly get to the stage to take my position because, along with my guitar, I had this huge, heavy guitar amp that I needed to bring with me. You could hear a pin drop in that audition room as I struggled to get all my gear to the stage. Once I finally got situated, I broke the deafening silence that covered the audition room with some ear-piercing feedback that came from plugging my guitar into the amplifier. As far as I could tell, I sure was making a great impression! I remember I wore a fuzzy, leopard print cowboy hat, a white sleeveless button-down blouse, black capri pants, with leopard print high-heeled platform sandals to match. See, Danny? Apparently, I *can* remember details when I want to. ☺

The schtick worked, because just a few short months later, in addition to performing on the sidelines of Texas Stadium, I found myself performing with the DCC show group as part of their complex dance show complete with elaborate costume changes. Remember when I said I was often in the back for the dance routines? Well, on USO tours, between dance numbers was my time to shine! That's when I would come out to sing a song, or to do some improvisational crowd work and interviews with the military men and women. Cheering at the Cowboys games was fun, but those moments entertaining the troops, in addition to traveling to fifteen or so different countries that year, were my fondest memories of being a Dallas Cowboys Cheerleader.

Thanks for walking, ahem, strutting with me down memory lane, but let's leave the bright lights of Texas Stadium and head back to the bright lights of my *Idol* audition. Kelly went to sing in front of the judges before I did. How would you like to be the girl who auditioned *after* Kelly Clarkson? Yeesh. Had to muster up more of that Texas-sized courage and act as if I was talented enough to be there too.

My number was called, and I walked into the iconic *American Idol* audition room. I remember seeing several large production cameras on tripods, silhouettes of people with walkie talkies and headsets watching from the wings, and there, about twenty feet in front of me, sat Randy Jackson, Paula Abdul, and Simon Cowell behind a long card table covered with a black tablecloth and a plastic blue-and-white sign hanging from the front that read "American Idol."

The first-season budget was exactly what you'd expect.

They broke the ice by asking me a few questions, and then it was time to perform my audition song. I chose "Fallin'" by Alicia Keys. I later learned that song selection is crucial, and looking back, I should've picked a song that better suited my vocal capability. But had I done so, what happened next wouldn't have been nearly as profound.

After I finished singing, I stood there, anxiously awaiting the judges' decisions. To make it through to the next round, I needed two out of the three of them to vote in favor of sending me to Hollywood. To my surprise, all three agreed! Once Paula declared, "You're going to Hollywood!" I proceeded to run to the judges table to give them all a hug and a firm Texas handshake, but at the last second, I slipped and fell, landing flat on my back.

Did you catch that? I sang "Fallin'" and *then I fell.* Please sit back and let the irony of that little scenario settle in for a quick minute. It's the stuff that sitcom writers' dreams are made of, and it happened to me in real life.

To make matters worse, the momentum of my run toward the table, combined with the weight of my fall, caused me to slide underneath the judges' table. I'm here to tell you that force really does equal mass times acceleration. I came in like a wrecking ball.

After the fall, I couldn't get up right away. I was trying to process what on earth had just happened. I lay there on my back, in a gigantic pool of my own embarrassment, staring at the ceiling with my arms stretched out in a T position, and didn't move for what felt like an eternity. Also, at this point, my feet were literally touching Paula's. I mean, straight up now, tell me, how did this even happen? As I contemplated how to get up and exit the room without anyone noticing, suddenly I saw Simon's face peer over the edge of the table. Through his laughter, he asked me with his signature snarky yet playful tone and famous British accent, "Are you okay?" And then, thankfully, Randy came around from behind the table and graciously helped me up.

As I left the room for the postaudition interview with Seacrest, I thought, "Wait a minute. Maybe no one will even watch this show. I mean, what are the chances that this will end up becoming the number one hit show on Fox with millions of people across America watching? Yeah, I have nothing to worry about. It'll probably be a flop."

Cut to the clip of my fall being repeatedly used in the special editions of "Idol's Most Embarrassing Moments."

After that point in the audition, the rest of the day is hazy to me. Between the sting of both the embarrassment and the actual fall, I didn't have room in my brain to process anything else. I remember the producers from the show telling me that they would be in touch in the coming weeks regarding the next round of the competition, which would take place in Los Angeles. Next up were the grueling "Hollywood Week" rounds, but until then, I went back to school until I received further instructions from the show.

Weeks later, I was lying in bed in my dorm room watching *Access Hollywood*. Back then it was hosted by Nancy O'Dell. I remember her coming onto the screen, then seeing the *American Idol* logo and hearing the show's theme song for the first time. My heart raced as I came to grips with the fact that this show was really happening. I don't remember exactly what Nancy said, but it was something along the lines of, "There's a new singing-competition show coming out on Fox. Check out this girl. She sang 'Fallin" and then she fell!"

My heart stopped racing and dropped straight to the floor. I thought, "Dear God, please tell me that someone else also sang 'Fallin" and then fell!" But, no. Alas, here I came onto the screen. I saw myself for the first time on national television, and for a few seconds it was great. I think I held my breath throughout the entire segment and was just waiting for the painful moment to arrive so I could exhale at some point. Waiting to see myself fall down on national television was like watching the movie *Titanic*. You can't fully enjoy watching the entire story play out because you know the horrific ending is imminent. You're just waiting for the ship to sink or, in my case, for the girl to fall.

To add insult to injury, *Access Hollywood* played my fall on a loop, about three times in a row. Or maybe that is just how I remember it. In any case, so began my "fifteen minutes of fame." Strangers approached me for several years after that, all asking the same question: "Excuse me. Are you the girl who fell down on *American Idol?*"

Yep. That's me.

The Hollywood Week rounds of competition are truly a blur. I remember getting little to no sleep, almost losing my voice due to the extreme amount of singing and rehearsals, and a lot of non-stop shuttling by the show's producers from one place to the next.

There were 121 contestants at the start of the week, and by the end the group would be down to the top thirty finalists. Right before they made final cuts to announce the top thirty, I had a decision to make.

Remember the pageant I won? Well, after winning a city title, I was scheduled to compete in the Miss Texas state competition during the same summer that *Idol* was filming. However, one of the contractual stipulations for the show is that contestants can't participate in any other televised competition-based events at the same time, which meant that to continue in the competition on *Idol*, I would have to forego my shot at winning Miss Texas. So during Hollywood Week, with the cameras rolling, Simon asked me what my decision was, the pageant or the show. I told him that I wanted to sing, and he replied, "I think you're a star."

While that was a flattering compliment to receive, because of the incredible amount of talent present that season, I feel like I shouldn't have made it past the first day of Hollywood Week. But again, I acted as if I was supposed to be there, and somehow, someway, I managed to slip my way into the top thirty. Literally.

Now it was time for those of us remaining in the competition to perform on the big stage in front of a live studio audience. My initial plan was to play guitar and sing "Cowboy Take Me Away," just as I had done for my Dallas Cowboys Cheerleader audition, but back then *Idol* didn't permit contestants to play instruments on the show. In fact, at that point, there wasn't even a full band, just piano accompaniment. The show wasn't yet the juggernaut that it would become, so everything was much more stripped down.

Also, the approved list of songs we had to select from was extremely limited due to music licensing costs, so I opted to sing "Fallin'" again.

I know, you think I would've learned my lesson. While I loved that song, I had no business trying to sing it, because loving a song doesn't necessarily mean you should *perform* that song.

On television.

In front of millions of people.

If you've watched *Idol* enough, you've probably heard the judges talk about how crucial a contestant's song selection is to their success in the competition. My initial plan of "Cowboy Take Me Away," or something in that vein, would've been a much better choice, but I plowed ahead, acted as if, and sang "Fallin'" for a second time on the show.

After my performance, as I stood there listening to the judges' critiques, I knew this was likely going to be the end of the road for me. Verbatim, Simon told me, "If I were judging a beauty competition, then you would win. But this is a singing competition, and you're out of your league." A classic Simon Cowell backhanded compliment for the win!

After my top thirty performance, they cut the contestants down from thirty finalists to ten, and that's when I went home. So I always tell people that I'm number eleven from season one of *American Idol*, because, hey, I could've been! Okay, technically there were backup selections known as "wild cards," so maybe I was more like number fifteen, but either way . . . I'll take it.

If I have any wisdom to share from my experience on a reality television show, it's that things aren't always as they seem. There is invariably more to someone's story. The power of media and the magic of editing can portray a myriad of narratives, so you have to diligently search for the truth these days and not be so quick to judge someone or a situation.

Because the show knew that I had given up the opportunity to compete in the Miss Texas pageant for a shot at competing on *Idol*, the producers chose to make that a featured part of my "story." I was portrayed as the "pageant, cheerleader girl from Texas," despite my ever competing in only one pageant and essentially faking my way into cheering—which, by the way, if you're going to do that, you should definitely choose the one pro sports team everyone knows for its cheerleaders.

Okay, thanks for coming to my TED Talk.

In any case, after the show I headed back to Texas to finish up my junior year of college, thinking my days on *Idol* were over forever.

Until . . .

Several weeks later, I read in the paper that *Idol* executives had decided not to bring back the cohost from season one and that Ryan Seacrest would be hosting season two solo. I immediately did what any ambitious Texas girl would do. I picked up the phone, called one of the executive producers, and asked if he would consider hiring someone else to cohost alongside Seacrest. He asked who I had in mind, and I confidently replied, "Me, of course!" I completely acted as if I was the obvious choice for the job. You know, the girl who's minimal on-camera television experience included falling down!

To my surprise, he sounded mildly intrigued, so I thought I may have a chance of talking him into this crazy idea—until, unfortunately, he wisely asked if I had any actual on-camera hosting experience. Hmmm, let me see. The only quasi experience I could think of were some segments I had filmed for a local morning show in Dallas as an *"American Idol* expert." I would give my predictions on the remaining top ten contestants from season one, and they'd air it because I'd been on the show. Surprisingly, he asked if he could see the footage. I couldn't believe it! We hung up, and I immediately called the local television station, got the tape, and overnighted the footage to him.

The actual tape. On VHS. If you don't know what that is, google it.

Three days later, thanks to divine providence and two associate producers who were in my corner encouraging the execs to give me a chance, I was sent an offer to cohost the audition episodes of *American Idol* season two, with an option to continue for the duration of the show if things worked out.

I sat there holding the phone and wondered, "Did this really just happen?" Had I just talked my way into cohosting the second season of the number one show on Fox, with *zero* television hosting experience? I truly believe this opportunity was divine intervention, because logically, it didn't make any sense. On the other hand, because of my lovely audition as a contestant, maybe they were banking on my doing something embarrassing again to help ratings.

The point is, you never know unless you ask. The worst someone can say is no.

My duties on the second season were to begin right away. I went from living in a twelve-by-twelve-foot dorm room at TCU to staying at a fancy suite at the Ritz Carlton in Detroit, the first audition city for season two. A car service picked me up from the Detroit airport, and flowers and tasty treats awaited me in my hotel room. How was this my life? Even today it all still feels like a dream.

For the next few months, I lived on the road with Paula, Simon, Randy, Ryan, and the *American Idol* production crew. Since I was now officially part of the crew and no longer just a hopeful contestant, I stayed in incredible hotels, was treated to dinner at exquisite restaurants, and had my hair and makeup professionally done on set every day. I'm not gonna lie—I felt like a princess. This sure did beat college life.

Kristin and Ryan Seacrest on the set of American Idol season 2, 2002.

One of my favorite memories from that time (for some reason I remember it in vivid detail) was shoe shopping with Paula in New York City. When we were there for auditions, the two of us went shopping one day in the famous SoHo district. We walked into a high-end shoe store, which has since closed its doors, called Otto Tootsi Plohound. I know. I think it's German for "You have to have money to shop here." Now, although I was the cohost of *American Idol*, I was definitely not making Seacrest-level money. Yet there I was, shopping with an A-list celebrity on a Z-list budget. I could already hear the sounds of creditors calling me for payment on the overpriced, one-of-a-kind, knee-high boots I was about to purchase.

It was my first of many experiences witnessing what life is like as a celebrity. The store employees were over-the-top nice to us. It took us twice as long as the average person to make a purchase, due to all the photo ops Paula graciously stopped to take with fans. It was a strange feeling knowing your every move was being

Kristin and Paula Abdul enjoying a night out in Los Angeles, 2003.

taken in and dissected through the eyes of onlookers from every angle. The sounds of cameras clicking seemed to never stop, as the paparazzi were outside with their superzoom camera lenses plastered against the boutique windows. I don't remember all that Paula purchased that day, but I do remember the ridiculously expensive, hand-painted, brown suede stiletto boots that I took home. I think I wore those puppies maybe twice, and at some point they made their way to a local Goodwill.

After that experience, I lived in LA working as a television host for fifteen years, and from my time spent at red-carpet events and press junkets and being in and around celebrity culture, I can say with confidence that none of us were built to withstand the trappings that come with fame. As my faith has grown, I've realized that the glory directed the way of famous people was always meant to be directed toward God. When we receive the weight of the glory He deserves, it ultimately destroys us. Only when we learn to deflect it and give it back to Him do we have

29

a fighting chance of successfully surviving the elusive platforms of fame and fortune.

Now, I'd like to take a moment here to address something that you may have wondered when I mentioned that I was hired to cohost season two of *Idol*. If you thought to yourself, "Wait a minute, Kristin. I don't remember seeing two hosts on *American Idol*." That's because my part was mostly cut out of the audition episodes before they aired on television, and I had a minimal role for the duration of the season—nowhere near cohosting responsibilities. Yeah, it hurt. I'm still in therapy for that one.

Of course, there were the obvious feelings of humiliation that came with being let go, but there were also some incredible blessings that came out of my time on the second season, and I'm extremely grateful for all the opportunities my experience with *Idol* afforded me. Originally, I was planning to move to Los Angeles once the show opted to pick me up for the second season, but since that didn't pan out, I now had no job awaiting me there. I didn't have a job, but thanks to *Idol*, I did have a Hollywood agent and my SAG card (which is vital for booking industry work). Now all I needed was a place to stay, but rent in LA isn't exactly affordable, especially when you're freshly unemployed.

I thought my time in Tinseltown had come to an end, until Paula generously offered me a place to stay while I figured out what my next steps would be. Paula . . . as in *Abdul*! My childhood idol had just asked me to be roommates. I mean, she's a legitimate celebrity, and I had fifteen minutes of fame on a reality show. But, hey, opposites attract, right?

I told her that I'd think about it for a few days, and then . . . are you kidding me? I moved my stuff into her place faster than a cold-hearted snake! Sorry, corny finds me like peanut butter finds jelly. It's just who I am.

So, thanks to Paula, who's forever my girl (okay, I'll stop) and an agent who sent me out to audition every day, I managed to successfully launch a fifteen-year television hosting career.

Here are some quick fun facts about my time in LA:

- I joined an indie pop band called Stranger Days, and we played gigs around the city, including famous spots on Sunset Strip. I worked with amazing musicians and producers and had the chance to meet with several record labels. It was an exhilarating time, but ultimately, it wasn't where I was supposed to be.
- I was one of Lindsay Lohan's backup singers during her *Speak* album tour in 2005 and performed alongside her on *The Ellen DeGeneres Show* and "Dick Clark's New Year's Rockin' Eve." I found myself whisked across the country to sing at music festivals and on television programs.
- I became a television host and correspondent for ten years on the G4TV network on shows like *Cheat!*, *Attack of the Show!*, and *X-Play*. I didn't know much about the gaming world when I started, but I learned as I went and, of course, acted as if. I was essentially a utility host that the network could plug in wherever they needed.
- I hosted shows and contributed work as a special correspondent on networks like Starz, Speed, USA Network, AT&T U-verse Buzz, E! Entertainment, and the TV Guide Channel. I never knew what type of work was going to be thrown my way. I learned to be prepared for anything and to think on my feet since most of the broadcasts were live

and there were no retakes or do-overs. Things didn't always go as planned, but as they say, the show must go on!

- A lot of my days in LA were spent on red carpets, at press junkets, or on TV or movie sets interviewing Hollywood casts and crews. Some of my all-time favorite interviews were with Matt Damon, Will Smith, and Betty White. Oh, and Elmo! The day I spent doing a behind-the-scenes look on the set of *Sesame Street* was surreal. I learned to listen and be responsive. My best interviews were when I was fully present, engaged, and listening to the answers given, not just planning what I was going to say next.

So there you have it. I was one of the hardest-working cable television hosts that you had probably never heard of! Hosting shows afforded me some of the most incredible experiences of my life, and I'm forever grateful to have had those opportunities, not least of all for everything they taught me, which prepared me to face what was to come . . .

Kristin on the red carpet at the Hollywood Awards interviewing for Starz! Network, 2011.

Kristin interviewing Usher at a red-carpet event in Hollywood, 2011.

Michael Kovac/WireImage/Getty Images

CHAPTER 3

THE FRIEND ZONE

Kristin: After the dust cleared from my stint on
American Idol and I moved to LA full-time
to pursue a television hosting career, that's
when we started hanging out more on a
semiregular basis.

Danny: Yeah. We had the same network of
friends, so we would see each other at get-
togethers and house parties.

Kristin: We still had a lot to learn about each
other at that point in time, but one thing we
knew early on is that we both had a lot of fun
when we were together.

Danny: Yes, we definitely made each other laugh,
and conversation with you was always easy.

Kristin: And shortly thereafter is when—how do I
put this?—my downward spiral began.

Danny: As your friend and someone who cared
about you, that was hard to watch.

Kristin

Within three months of living in LA, I had lost myself. And it wasn't because smartphones with GPS didn't exist at this point in time. Hello, Thomas Guide! I obviously knew where I was in the physical sense. But I had become a version of myself that was so far off from the girl I had always known. This responsible and ambitious Texas girl with a "good head on her shoulders" somehow started making one foolish decision after another. I thought I knew who I was, but my spiritual and ideological roots weren't as deep as I had thought. Someone somewhere once said that self-deception is the worst kind of deception. During that season of my life, I found that to be true. I thought I could handle the nightlife and seductiveness of Hollywood and resist being pulled in too far. I mean, professionally, things couldn't have been going better. I was auditioning and booking industry jobs left and right. But personally, things were becoming increasingly unhealthy and destructive, more so than I realized at the time. For starters, I was going out and partying almost every night of the week. One drink led to two drinks. Two drinks led to three drinks. Three drinks . . . you get the idea.

And in LA, going out is so much more of "a scene" than in most other cities because celebrities are involved. The popular clubs typically hire the best nightclub promoter in town, who then ensures that certain celebrities will attend, which in turn creates long lines of people outside waiting to get in, just so they can say they were at the same place as so-and-so. Sometimes there aren't even that many people inside the building, but the goal is simply to create the facade with the long lines that *this* is the place to be, and eventually the place fills up. The lines are typically filled with throngs of young people doing their best to look good enough to impress the door guy. He's the gatekeeper. If you're not on "the list" or you don't "look the part," then the door guy isn't going to let you in. So in LA, you not only spend your days auditioning for parts you'll most likely never get, you then also spend your nights "auditioning" to get into clubs you'll likely never get into either. It's an exhausting and expensive hamster wheel of defeat.

But, oh, when you *do* book the gig or get into the club and sit two booths down from that somebody from that one show that everyone knows, you feel like you are sitting on top of the world. You feel like you have made it. Because most of the Western world revolves around Hollywood. At least that's what people in Hollywood think. And that's not an entirely unfounded thought. I mean, if we're basing that premise on the amount of time and money we as a society spend on buying whatever Hollywood is selling, then the idea does hold some water.

The presence of celebs is not the only thing that adds to the excitement of nightlife in LA. There are all kinds of young Hollywood types everywhere you turn, and getting attention from them can become intoxicating and addicting. I fell into this trap and quickly realized, after being used a time or two or three, that I was never intended as their next relationship. I was simply their next shiny object. If there ever was an e-course on training folks in the ways of seeking the next shiny object, then living in Hollywood would be a real-life master class. To make things worse, not only did I allow people to use me, I started using people.

That's the collateral damage of the next-shiny-object syndrome: people.

You're never enough. Other people are never enough. Nothing satisfies. You begin living for the short-term praise, attention, and validation from others, when really, all that matters is the audience of One. But unfortunately, I didn't realize that back then. I hurt not only myself during that season, but I hurt a lot of other people as well.

Danny

I had seen stories like Kristin's play out many times in the year I lived out there before she arrived. I had witnessed a trend in LA that when people from Anywhere, USA, would arrive there to pursue their dreams, if they didn't have a strong sense of identity, purpose, and conviction when they arrived, they would ultimately find themselves in compromising positions. I always had a big-brother heart for K, and I was heartbroken to see her going down this path, but I wasn't in a position to "preach" because I wasn't exactly walking the straight and narrow path myself. I was in and out of church and more focused on chasing my dreams than chasing after God.

As Kristin shared, there's an unhealthy relational cycle that one can easily fall into in LA. It's a city full of ego, and unless you're in a position to help someone fulfill their dreams, they aren't going to give you the time of day. For example, I would always notice that eye contact during conversations was rare. Often whomever I'd be speaking to would be looking over my shoulder to see if someone else more important had walked into the room. Once they realized that I couldn't help their career or offer them access to someone who could, then they were completely uninterested in me and moved on to the next person. So, to say the least, relationships can be very shallow out there.

> **Kristin:** All that partying eventually caught up with me in more ways than one—mentally, emotionally, relationally, spiritually, and physically. I had put on a little extra weight from pounding so many Jack and Cokes, followed by late-night trips to greasy fast-food joints, so I called you for some personal training to get back into shape.
>
> **Danny:** Yeah, while I moved to LA to pursue comedy, my livelihood for many years was personal fitness training.
>
> **Kristin:** Anyone in our circle of friends who could afford a trainer went to you for help.
>
> **Danny:** I love fitness and I love people, so it was a natural fit for me. It honestly never felt like a job.

Danny

Fitness and sports were always a big part of my life. When I was growing up, God was first in my family, but sports were a close second. When we weren't at church, we were most likely at a sporting event or watching one at home. My father encouraged us to stay active all year round and was often our coach throughout Little League. I was a three-sport athlete and was blessed to have success and great experiences from the time I started playing. I loved every sport I played, but football grew to be my favorite. Playing in the NFL was always a dream of mine, and I worked extremely hard to try and make that happen. I left nothing on the field, as they say. Once I began college, my summer training regimen consisted of long training hours lifting weights, running sprints, and pushing my 1989 Chevy Celebrity up and down the street. For all you football fanatics, it was Mike Alstott–style, baby! A.k.a. "A-Train"!

While I spent a lot of time involved in sports, anytime the church doors were open, my family and I were in attendance. There were the Tuesday night "back door" gatherings where we met for games and fellowship, the Wednesday night prayer meetings, and of course the Sunday services, both morning and night. Now *that* was the Lawd's Day! My family took our relationships with Jesus seriously. We rarely missed church, but when did, we were on the road ministering at other churches as singing evangelists.

> **Kristin:** Now, if like me, you've never heard of singing evangelists, that's when people travel around to different churches and sing gospel music. When Danny told me that he and his family traveled as singing evangelists, the only vision that came to my mind was of them going door-to-door, like a Christian singing telegram of sorts. As in, "Hello, my darlin', hello, my honey, have you heard about my friend, Jesus?" Honestly, I had no clue. All I could think of were groups like the Osmonds, the Partridge family, the Von Trapp family, and so on. Okay, continue, babe.

Danny

As the youngest of three kids, I was birthed into a singing evange-list family. As teenagers, my dad and his brother, along with some friends of theirs, started a singing quartet called The Revelators. On the other side of town, my mom was busy singing with a female group from her church, The Westside Trio, and happened to be a fan of The Revelators. Apparently, Mom had a thing for men in plaid blazers and crew cuts, and she especially liked the way Dad "wiggled his leg when he sang." She also likes to say, "Your father rolled his eyes at me from stage, and I just picked them up and rolled 'em right back." Their odd way of flirting seemingly worked, because fifty-four years later, they are still going strong. Dad says the key to a successful marriage is going on a date night twice a week. An ordinary restaurant doesn't cut

The Jerry Adams Family gospel group, 1987. From left: David (Danny's brother), Jerry (Danny's dad), Allene, (Danny's mom), Dawn (Danny's sister), Danny (center).

it. It has to be upscale and low lit, with elegant ambiance and impeccable service. When I asked Dad if they've really done that twice a week for fifty-four years, he said, "Absolutely. I go on Tuesdays; your Mom goes on Fridays. It works out perfectly."

Shortly after they were married, they formed their own group, called The Lighthouse Quartet. Years later, after a few changes in group members, their name changed to Heaven's Happy Sounds. Yep, you heard that right.

Fast-forward several years later, and my two siblings and I joined the group, which was thankfully now called The Jerry Adams Family. We all played different instruments—I was the drummer—and we sang harmony together as a family. Eventually, this family act evolved into a variety show that included songs and skits. This was where I found my niche, working on my early sketch-comedy craft and developing original characters. I saw at a young age what laughter did for people, that it truly was medicine. There were many instances after performing with my family when various people prophetically spoke to me, saying that God was going to use my gift of inciting laughter for His glory. I was always so encouraged by this, and I knew that after my football days came to an end, I would likely pursue a career in comedy and entertainment.

But first I had to give my dream of playing in the NFL my best shot. It was a dream I'd had since I was seven years old. After I finished playing ball in college as a two-time NAIA All-American Honorable Mention, a handful of NFL teams started to show some interest. NFL scouts came to my college to put me through workouts. I tested well, specifically in the categories of speed and strength. My field stats as a tight end, along with my versatility as a quarterback and special teams player, combined with my strong test results from the scout workouts, "raised my stock" as they say in the world of sports recruitment. Even so, I knew there was no possibility of being drafted from a lower-level NAIA school. At this point, my best chance was to be signed as a free agent to training camp, with the hopes of eventually making it onto a team.

So you can imagine my excitement when I received a phone call from the tight ends coach of the Cincinnati Bengals the night before the NFL draft, asking me to "stay by the phone," because there was a chance they would bring me in as a free agent depending on how their draft picks went the next day. Then the NFL carrot was dangled even more, because the following morning, I received a call from the Tennessee Titans' special teams coach, essentially repeating the same thing that the Bengals coach told me. I held my breath for the next few days as the NFL draft came to an end, hoping to receive a phone call.

That call never came.

After that, I had a couple of conversations with coaches from other NFL teams encouraging me to stay in shape and be ready to go, as the NFL season is long and can be full of injuries. So I kept up with my workouts throughout that season and into the next upcoming draft, once again hoping to land with a team through free agency. Long story short, it ended up being a rinse and repeat of the year before. I received interest from teams like the Minnesota Vikings and Tampa Bay Buccaneers, but at the end of the day, there were no official offers or invites on the table.

I was devasted, to say the least. I went through a couple of years after that where I was mad at God and confused as to why He didn't allow my childhood dream to come to pass. Of course, I now see His hand in it all and know that regardless of the course my life takes, His plans are always better than my own. (That being said, if there are any teams out there that are still interested, my phone number hasn't changed.)

While my NFL dreams were done, my football days didn't come to an end just yet. Years later, I had the opportunity to play for a couple of seasons overseas in the European Football League for teams in Switzerland, Austria, and the Czech Republic. Yes, American football does exist in other parts of the world, though it definitely is not as popular as it is in the States. For me, this was one of the most exciting and enjoyable times in my life. I was once again playing a game that I absolutely love while simultaneously soaking up some incredible cultures and seeing beautiful parts of the world.

But eventually it was time for me to hang up the cleats and head for Hollywood, hopefully to fulfill those prophesies from those sweet church folks all those years ago. After getting my LA starter kit together—headshots, agent, acting classes—I hit the ground running and ran around town auditioning for anything I could, from acting roles to fitness modeling and stunt work for sports sequences in commercials, TV shows, and movies.

Danny playing quarterback for the St. Gallen Vipers in Switzerland, 2004.

Here's some quick highlights of some of my favorite industry jobs I had the opportunity to do during my time in LA:

- Stunt double for Peyton Manning twice—once in a Gatorade commercial and once for a comedy sketch on the Nickelodeon Kids' Choice Awards. Since I'm from Indianapolis, this was especially cool for me as I've always had the utmost respect for Peyton both on and off the field.

- Stunt double for Drew Brees in an NFL/Microsoft commercial.

- Spartan soldier for the movie *300*. Well, let me clarify. Many of the computer-generated soldiers on the battlefield were based off a mold from my body, so that counts, right?

- Featured background actor (a personal trainer, to be exact!) on *The Young and the Restless*. To this day, I enter most rooms with a slow and dramatic walk. ☺

Danny on set at the LA Memorial Coliseum, doubling NFL New Orleans Saints quarterback Drew Brees for an NFL/Microsoft commercial shoot, 2016.

- Football stunt work in *Key and Peele* comedy sketches on Comedy Central, and in commercials for brands like Old Spice, Dick's Sporting Goods, Coca-Cola, Nike, and Pepsi.

- Basketball stunt work and stunt coordinating for the movie *Underclassman*.

While those years of auditioning and filming were a blast, my work was often sporadic and inconsistent, so my main livelihood during that time was personal fitness training. After working for a couple of small neighborhood gyms in Studio City and North Hollywood, I eventually opened my own private training studio. Having my own training business afforded me the flexibility to take auditions when they would come up and adjust my training hours accordingly when I booked gigs.

Danny: I was excited when you called for some fitness training, and I just so happened to have an eight o'clock slot on Tuesdays and Thursdays open.

Kristin: I could only afford a couple of days per week because you weren't cheap!

Danny: And that was even with the pretty-girl discount.

Kristin: Okay! (snaps)

Danny: I could've filled that spot at full price with "Dad-Bod Dave." But I opted to start my morning with something a little easier on the eyes.

Kristin: Well, I'm grateful for the pretty-girl discount because without it, we may have never happened.

Danny: That's true. Our training sessions were where our friendship really took off.

Kristin: Yeah, because you tell your trainer everything, like you do your hair stylist. But had I known we would eventually be getting

married, I wouldn't have told you anything!
I would've kept my mouth shut on Tuesday
and Thursday mornings.

Danny: It's okay, babe. Your secrets are safe
with me. But I mean, yes, I did file everything
away in my mental Rolodex . . . in case I ever
needed it.

Kristin: Hey, love keeps no record of wrongs,
remember?

Danny: True, but I gathered that information
before we fell in love.

Kristin: Well, poop. So then eventually I had my
"breakdown" outside the gym.

Danny: Probably about six months in or so . . .
I remember we had just finished a session,
and I walked you outside toward your car,
and we stood there for a bit, making small
talk before you left.

Kristin: I was telling you that my younger brother
was coming to town later that day to hang
with me in LA for the week.

Danny: Yeah, and as you were telling me, you
suddenly got a little choked up and teary-
eyed, explaining how you were nervous to
have him around because you had changed
so much since you'd last seen him.

Kristin: I was always the older sister with the
good head on her shoulders, and now I
had turned into this version of myself that
was difficult even for me to recognize. My

drinking was borderline out of control, I had started smoking regularly, and my "friendships" at that point were all centered on going out and partying every night. I emotionally unloaded on you that day, and I remember thinking, as I was crying and trying to explain everything, how much I valued your friendship in that moment. At the time, you were pretty much the only decent guy I knew.

Danny: So obviously that's when I made my move. You were so emotional and vulnerable, I pulled you in close, your sweat and tears rolling down my tank top.

Kristin: That's just like you! Gotta go and be the funny guy as I'm baring my soul.

Danny: Well, whatever I did worked that day, because your breakdown ended with you asking if I'd hang out with you and your brother that night.

Kristin: Yep, and I've regretted that invite to this day.

Danny: Ouch.

Kristin

Even with all the early success I was having in Hollywood, I still felt empty and unfulfilled. In my dating life, I jumped from one "fling" to the next and was caught up in the dangerous hookup culture that has unfortunately become so commonplace.

I was feeling the insurmountable weight of the emptiness and loneliness that my lifestyle choices had caused, and those feelings came to a head that day outside Danny's gym. The realization that I had a phone full of hundreds of contacts—including celebrities, "the guy I met at Sky Bar that one Tuesday night," and everyone in between—hit me like a ton of bricks. I even told Danny out loud that if I died tomorrow, I felt like no one in my LA life would probably even notice. That's how kiddie-pool-deep most of my relationships were at that point.

Now that my younger brother was coming to visit, I was more self-aware of my life and circumstances and began to look at myself through his eyes. Sure, I was excited to show him the television set I got to work from and take him to red-carpet events, but at the end of the day, I wanted him to know that his big sister was winning in the areas that truly mattered. But I didn't have much to show him in the way of healthy relationships and personal life choices. I meant it when I said Danny was the only decent guy I knew back then. Even though he wasn't "walking with the Lord" at that time either, I was still drawn to his kindness, goodness, and decency, and I made up my mind, right then and there, that I wanted him to spend time with my brother and me that week.

Danny: The night that your brother got into town, you guys picked me up and we cruised around the city, showing him some of our favorite local spots, including a once-famous record store in LA on Hollywood Boulevard called Amoeba Music. And then over the course of the next few days, we hit some of the more standard tourist attractions, like the Grove and Hollywood & Highland, went to a Dodgers game, and made some great memories.

Kristin: Are you going to mention the part when we drove down to Santa Monica to see you at your weekend gig as the door/security/bouncer guy at that restaurant bar place where you got my underage brother in through the back door?

Danny: Uh . . . no, I wasn't.

Kristin: Oh, sorry. Continue.

Danny: I was going to skip the illegal part, but now that you brought it up, we actually had a lot of fun that night. We stood by the back door and talked and laughed for hours.

Kristin: That's when the official flirting between us started.

Danny: It was like a literal switch that night! We went from just friends to full-on puppy love.

Kristin: Nothing like a little illegal activity to get the flirtation ball rolling.

Danny: You make it sound like we robbed a bank. All I did was slip your brother into the back door of a restaurant that served adult beverages.

Kristin: Hey, illegal is illegal. Sin is sin.

Danny: Anywhoo, that night, after I got off work, we went to Denny's to grab a bite to eat, and I don't think we all left to go home until four in the morning or so. I remember driving on an empty 405 freeway, thinking of you and how much fun we just had and also thinking, "Wait a minute . . . what just happened between K and me?"

Kristin: And then shortly after we left, I called you within a few minutes.

Danny: I answered and said, "Funny you should call . . ."

Kristin: And I said, "Why's that?"

Danny: And I said, "Ah, I'll tell you later."

Kristin: And I said, "Well, you've already waited three years. How long is it gonna take?"

Danny: I sort of laughed that comment off but thought, "I just officially got the green light, baby!"

Kristin: The day my brother flew back home, you and I had our first real date that night.

Danny: July 15, 2005.

Kristin: And then you proposed exactly three years later on July 15, 2008.

Danny: Whoa, you can't jump ahead three whole years! You're skipping all the good stuff.

Danny

Because of our three years of trusted friendship, once we opened the door to dating each other, things between us moved fairly quickly. At the time, I was working ten to twelve hours each day at the gym and would spend any free time that I did have with

K. I was barely getting any sleep during those first few months we were together, but I didn't care. No matter how tired I was, the very thought of seeing her gave me a new surge of energy. I planned something fun and new for us to do just about every weekend. We did everything from seeing Tony Bennett in concert at the Hollywood Bowl and Michael Bublé at the Greek Theatre to taking day trips and driving up the famous Highway 1 coastline, exploring popular spots along the way, like Solvang, Morro Bay, San Simeon, and Hearst Castle.

When we weren't out having an adventure or painting the town, we were enjoying late-night conversations and dance sessions in the living room of Kristin's apartment in Studio City. Music has always been a huge part of our relationship, and we loved introducing each other to different artists and songs. For example, on our first date, I took her to see an R&B/soul artist named Kem, who sings some of the most silky-smooth love ballads out there. I knew that Kristin had never heard of him before, but I wanted to introduce her to a little bit of my world. She was up for going, and midway through the concert, Stevie Wonder made a surprise appearance and joined Kem on a couple of songs, playing his harmonica. When I saw that Kristin not only loved the music but was a Stevie fan too, I knew our first date was a success.

Kristin

So at this point, it's pretty clear that Danny is a romantic. His genuine kindness and thoughtful gestures were so refreshing after all the empty, shallow, unhealthy relationships I had just come out of for the past few years. I felt seen, pursued, and valued, and most importantly, I felt safe. Danny was loyal, and after the betrayal I had both perpetuated and received in many of my past relationships, this was a breath of fresh air. He was always bringing me homemade cards and fresh flowers and creating the perfect playlists for our road trips. Well, at the time it was more of a CD/mixtape situation, but nonetheless, he was always prepared with the perfect jams for whatever we were doing.

Kristin: While we were having a blast during those early dating months, you were still my personal trainer.

Danny: Well, if you would call it that.

Kristin: What do you mean?

Danny: K, you went from being so coachable in our sessions when we were just friends to so *not* coachable when we started dating.

Kristin: Well, now, you weren't just my trainer . . . you were my *boyfriend*.

Danny: Every time I would ask you to do a squat or a lunge, you thought for sure I was trying to tell you your butt was too big.

Kristin: That, yes, combined with the fact that every time you would come over to my place, you would leave behind other hints as well.

Danny: Like what?

Kristin: Like you swapped my frozen taquitos and corn dogs for frozen berries for smoothies, my sugary cereals for steel-cut, high-fiber oatmeal, and my powdered donuts for five huge jugs of flavored whey protein powder. If that doesn't make a girl feel insecure, I don't know what does!

Danny: Look, I saw a future with you, and I wanted you to live long enough to be a part of it.

Kristin: Ah, that's sweet. But give me back my donuts.

CHAPTER 4

THE MAN-TO-MAN TALK

Danny: Within five months of us dating, you took me to Texas to meet your parents.

Kristin: That was a big deal. My California boyfriend was coming home for the holidays.

Danny: I didn't realize how different our upbringings were until that first trip to Dallas.

Kristin: What? Your dad didn't make you sit through a hunting safety course on your thirteenth birthday?

Danny: Uh, no. Guns and camo were not a part of my childhood.

Kristin: That's too bad.

Danny: On top of that, you gave me zero heads-up on what I was about to walk into.

Kristin: Why would I give you a heads-up on something that was completely normal to me?

Danny: A fully stuffed mountain lion displayed with professional lighting on the landing of your entryway staircase? Yeah, that's completely normal.

Danny

Because we met while living in California, we were both excited to take each other back to our hometowns to meet our families and to see where we each grew up. I already loved Kristin at this point and saw an amazing future with her. That being said, I was eager to go to Texas and meet the people who could potentially become my future family. As K mentioned earlier, I'm a romantic at heart, and I always had lofty visions of one day meeting my in-laws, having secret handshakes, wearing matching sweaters, and hearing them laugh hysterically at all my jokes—even the ones they had heard several times before, because that's what family does. I couldn't wait to start making memories and sharing a lot of love and laughter together throughout the years.

Kristin

I wish I could say I shared Danny's enthusiasm with regard to him meeting my family. Considering my parents' reactions to my previous relationships, the odds of things going well were not in Danny's favor. My dad's idea of matching sweaters would've been him dressed in head-to-toe hunting gear and Danny dressed as a target.

Don't get me wrong. My parents were always my biggest cheerleaders in any endeavor I pursued. They did everything in their power to encourage me to go after my goals and dreams. Because of them I truly believed I could achieve anything. But when it came to my relationship choices, they were far less supportive, which was understandable given that my dating history included a drug dealer and a narcissistic man who, shockingly, turned out to be married with three children and had another girlfriend on the side.

So on the rare occasion when I made a solid dating choice, my parentes were typically skeptical and would proceed with caution. Good luck, Danny!

Danny

As I walked into Kristin's parents' beautifully kept suburban home, I quickly realized I had entered the animal kingdom. There was wild game everywhere. As I stood in the foyer, I landed in the shadow of a large elk head, which hung directly over me. To my left, positioned to appear as if he were climbing down rocks toward me, was the full body of a stuffed mountain lion. Its fangs were exposed, and its big hungry eyes followed me everywhere I went, like a creepy 3D museum painting. Next was a tour of her father's home office, complete with a wild turkey mounted behind his desk, wings and feathers spread out, along with dozens of deer heads,

One of the many magnificent (and intimidating) pieces of taxidermy in Kristin's parents' home in North Dallas.

antlers, and other species of the forest this city boy is still unable to identify.

But wait, there's more. In the living room, a bobcat crawled along the fireplace mantel, and a rattlesnake lay across the top of the television. There was something called an aoudad, as well as more heads and antlers mounted in various places along the walls. I don't know if this next part was real or just in my head, but I also remember sound effects of the grasslands and forests coming from every direction.

Kristin

It's true. My father was an accomplished, avid hunter. To add to the intimidation, he was a decorated Marine sniper, with a Purple Heart to boot. So that explains why I sat through a six-hour hunting safety course on my thirteenth birthday. I'm the oldest sibling, so Dad was eager to finally have one of us legally able to hunt alongside him. After our first trip to the gun range, my father was elated to realize that his daughter was a natural shot. Just sayin'.

On our first hunting trip, the opportunity to shoot my first deer presented itself. We were out driving an old rugged, open-air, camouflaged vehicle on my dad's deer lease in south Texas when a majestic eight-point buck jumped out, roughly twenty yards in front of us. We slowly pulled to a stop, and I got down into position to take my shot. I looked through the scope of the gun, and that innocent buck stared straight back at me. His big, beautiful brown eyes just cut through the scope, seemingly begging for mercy. After what felt like an eternity, I asked my dad if he would be mad at me if I didn't shoot the deer. Of course, he said no, and from that point on, I accompanied him on several hunting trips, without my ever killing anything. While I enjoyed eating the venison stew my dad was famous for making, I could never bring myself to do the dirty work.

Danny: After just the first few minutes of being in your home, I quickly realized that I was out of my element. I didn't serve in the military, nor had I ever been hunting, or even shot a gun, for that matter. Plus, I'm an extreme extrovert, and your father was a man of few words.

Kristin: Yeah, the conversation didn't exactly flow.

Danny: I felt like I tried everything. I had questions on several topics, and all he gave me was either "Yep" or "Nope" in his distinct Southern drawl.

Kristin: Well, you weren't in the circle of trust yet.

Danny: Well, you didn't help much in that arena by asking me to perform characters and comedy bits around the dinner table that night.

Kristin: What?! I was just trying to put you in a position to do what you do best!

Danny: K, again, you gave me zero heads-up! I'm busy scarfing down your mom's delicious homemade lasagna, and you pipe up with, "Danny, be funny! Go on, do one of your characters!"

Kristin: I just wanted them to see how funny you are.

Danny: Babe, you can't force funny. Funny just happens. And telling a joke onstage is totally different from attempting to entertain people who didn't ask to be entertained. But now I was in the awkward position of not wanting to negate your request in front of your parents, who I'd just met three hours before, by the way, and I also didn't want to start performing at the dinner table without any prep or plan.

Kristin: Gotcha. Okay, now I know for next time. However, since I was unaware of all of that, I went ahead and suggested that you do one of your specific characters, named Jeremiahs. You read that correctly. Jeremiah with an s.

Danny: Yes, the super-hyper six-year-old boy with a lazy eye and a strong lisp.

Kristin: He wears a hat, and I thought I was helping by asking my brother to run upstairs and grab one of his for you to use.

Danny: Yes, thank you so much. That was very helpful.

Kristin: You're welcome.

Danny: So I reluctantly started doing this character. I did my best to commit and just push through. Meanwhile, you're the only one laughing, your brother's giving me courtesy chuckles, and Bentley, the family dog, is pathetically looking at me like, "Bro, you're bombing. Make it stop."

Kristin: Babe . . . is fifteen years too late to say
I'm sorry?

Danny: Yes. Anyhow, I was mortified and spent
the next couple of days saying very little.
Literally, I think the only time I opened my
mouth was to eat your mom's home-cooked
meals every few hours.

Kristin: Until you had the man-to-man talk with
Dad.

Danny: Right, but I said very little then too.

Danny

It was Sunday afternoon, day three of our visit, and Kristin and
her mom were off wrapping Christmas presents in another room,
leaving her father and me alone in the family room with the
Cowboys game on. Now, if it's a Sunday during football season
in Texas, then you best believe you're watching America's team
throw around the pigskin. I'm sitting in the middle of the couch,
and K's dad is watching as he paces back and forth from the
kitchen to the family room.

We both made a few small comments on the game, and I
think, "Man, if there's any area for her father and me to connect
on, it's gotta be sports." But in that moment, I realized he had
more on his mind than football. During the next commercial
break, he walked over to the couch, stood over me, looked down,
and said, "Son, it's about time you and I had a man-to-man talk."
I said, "Yes, sir," and went to stand up out of respect and to allow
him to have some room on the couch if he wanted to sit down.

But he quickly put his hand on my shoulder, sat me right back down, and said, "This won't take long."

Now before I go on, it's important to note that K's dad stood six feet tall, but he was six foot four if you counted his hair. This man had the greatest mane of hair I've ever seen. Most people lose their hair when they get older, but K's father somehow grew it. He was a real-life Chia Pet. Every time he showered, his hair got thicker and stronger. I swear his glorious hair helmet came equipped with a chin strap. I imagined him unbuckling it at night and carefully placing it on a mannequin head on his nightstand, well-lit, like the mountain lion.

He went on to say, "Danny, if you ever physically or emotionally hurt my daughter . . . I'll play." And he just let that statement marinate for a minute.

"'I'll play,'" I thought. "What does that even mean? Play football? Checkers? Freeze tag?"

But then, as I looked up at him and his gorgeous man hair, flanked by two deer heads, I suddenly thought, "Wait, am I the game?"

He finally broke the silence with, "But, son, if you treat her like I think you do, we'll be just fine."

As I gave a huge internal sigh of relief, he even went on to share some encouraging words about how he thought it was pretty neat that Kristin and I were out in Hollywood chasing our dreams together, and how if we ever needed anything, we should never hesitate to ask him.

Sadly, nine years later, K's dad died unexpectedly of a heart attack. That man-to-man talk was the longest and most meaningful conversation the two of us ever shared. And now that I'm a father of a young girl, I know exactly what "I'll play" means.

Kristin's dad, a.k.a. "G'Pa," reading with Harper, 2011.

CHAPTER 5

DYS*FUN*CTIONAL

Kristin: One of the biggest mistakes we made while we were dating was moving in together.

Danny: For sure . . . and we justified the decision all day long.

Kristin: For one, the lease on my apartment was coming to an end, and my roommate had temporarily relocated to another city.

Danny: And because I had to move out of my apartment complex due to mold, I'd been temporarily staying with my best friend, his wife, and their Labrador retriever in a tiny one-bedroom apartment and sleeping on their couch, so I was definitely ready for a change. Well, we were *all* ready for a change.

Kristin: Not to mention, you were pretty much staying at my place almost every night anyway, so we figured, hey, we're already basically living together, so what's the difference?

Danny: My brother called me during that time and tried to advise me against the decision, but I just didn't want to hear any kind of wisdom like that. You and I were already "playing house," so to speak, and it's hard to go backward once you're in that place.

Kristin: We were essentially trying to get all the blessings of being married—living together, sex, intimacy, oneness—without actually being married.

Danny: And we quickly found ourselves in a codependent mess of a relationship.

Danny

I didn't know much at all about codependency until my relationship with Kristin led me to do some research. *Codependency* in layman's terms means a reliance on other people for approval and sense of identity. In our case, I constantly tried to earn Kristin's approval, which was nearly impossible to get, and she was reliant upon me to meet her emotional needs.

When conflict would arise, we didn't have any healthy coping methods. We would get into a fight, then dump the last fight on top of the current fight, and so on and so forth. It was a crazy cycle that we couldn't seem to stop.

Needless to say, we had some epic fights during that season. Some were so bad that we even named them based on where they took place. There was "Hollywood Boulevard," "New York City," and even "Rome, Italy." That's right, we took our fights international!

In spite of our unhealthy relationship dynamics, the fact was that I loved Kristin. I just didn't have the right spiritual tools in my toolbox to fix things.

Kristin

Before we moved in together, nothing about Danny really bothered me. Once we moved in together, seemingly everything about him began to irritate me. It could be the simplest of things, like, for instance, how he loaded the dishwasher. Something as ridiculous as that would trigger me. I would open it up, see the unorganized mess of dishes and cups, and think, "What kind of idiot would load the dishwasher that way?" And sometimes there wasn't any reason at all; I was simply mad at him for the way I was feeling. If I was having a bad day, somehow it must've been Danny's fault.

I had experienced these types of unhealthy relationships before, but this was Danny's first time to experience anything like this. Back then I would say awful things in the heat of the moment and then expect Danny to be fine the next second, without any resolve or attempt at reconciliation. I wasn't quick to hand out apologies, as that would've meant admitting that I was in the wrong for something. And I never thought I was wrong about anything. Then, in the midst of our mess, Danny got the crazy idea that we should start going to church.

Danny

I knew that things with K and me had to change, or our relationship wasn't going to survive. One night, while we were visiting one of our favorite local frozen yogurt shops, a girl I knew but hadn't seen in a while approached us. She was beaming with joy and was carrying on about how God had changed her life. At the end of her testimony, she invited us to attend her church sometime. Now, growing up in a Christian family and attending church most of my life, I'd seen many people come to know Christ and witnessed the heart-change that would follow. So I knew right away that what I saw and heard from my friend at the yogurt shop was the real deal. I was instantly convicted, but because of Kristin's apparent lack of interest or enthusiasm, I had a feeling that a visit to that church probably wasn't going to happen. Plus, despite both of our upbringings of weekly Sunday school and church camps, neither of us mentioned God much to each other at that point, much less went to church.

For a couple of weeks, I couldn't stop thinking about the encounter at the yogurt shop, but I was nervous to bring up the idea of attending church to K. Nonetheless, I asked her.

Kristin

I said yes, but I honestly had zero desire to go to church with Danny. Prior to living in California, I'd been to church almost every week of my life. I mean, y'all, I grew up in the buckle of the Bible Belt, for cryin' out loud! Attending church always seemed like the right thing to do, and going made me feel good about myself, but I had yet to experience an authentic life-changing relationship with Christ. I have fond memories of attending candlelight Christmas services, singing old hymns, and playing games at church camp, which were all good experiences. Because of those experiences I had hope and seeds of faith deep down inside. But I still didn't see the point of going to church other than "it's just what you should do." Even if I was aware of the good news of the gospel at that point, and I understood it had the power to heal me from the inside out and put me in right standing with God, I wasn't really interested in changing anything about my life. I was pretty content with the way things were. The fights that Danny and I had didn't bother me as much as they bothered him—I mean, as long as I won them, of course.

Nonetheless, I got all gussied up that Sunday, and we headed off to church. I must say, I had never been to a church like this before. There were tons of people, and nearly all of them seemed *extra* happy. The greeters said things like, "Have a blessed day," and "Praise the Lord," and it was all just a bit much for me.

When we entered the sanctuary, I hoped to snag a couple of seats in the back in case we wanted to leave early, but the ushers quickly stepped in and sat us toward the front. The first twenty to thirty minutes of service was all music. I now know that's called "praise and worship," which was an entirely different experience than the choir with matching robes I was accustomed to at my church back in Texas. Many people closed their eyes as they sang, and some even put their hands in the air as if they were reaching toward heaven. I will say that the music was next-level amazing, even if I did feel out of my element.

Then the pastor got up for a forty-five-minute sermon, longer than I had ever heard any one person talk about Jesus at one time. I wasn't fully buying what he was selling, but I definitely respected his wisdom and preaching ability. At the end of the service, something happened that I'd never seen before. The pastor asked if anyone wanted to "receive eternal salvation by accepting Jesus into their heart" or to "rededicate their life to Christ." If so, they were invited to get out of their seats and come to the altar for prayer. Whaaat? People were going to stand up, in front of hundreds of strangers, and admit that they needed that? Nope, I'm fine, thank you very much.

But then suddenly, I felt *Danny* stand up next to me. I thought, "Dear God, please tell me he's just going to the bathroom!" But alas, Danny, the man I was planning to go home with that day, went forward to "rededicate" his life to Jesus. He not only went to the altar, but as he stood there waiting to receive prayer, he also was crying, with his hands lifted high. What did that even mean? How was this decision going to affect us? Was Danny going to be different now? Like, boring or something?

Thankfully, the service was finally over, and I was ready to make a beeline to the car. But instead, Danny made a beeline for the church bookstore. He bought what seemed like loads of faith-based books and Bible study materials, and then he started to inquire about volunteering and joining the men's ministry. You guys, he was basically wrestling serpents and speaking in tongues on the way to the parking lot. I mean, can we at least ease into this whole Jesus thing? Somebody help me!

The car ride was uncomfortably quiet all the way home. I had no idea what to say, and quite frankly, neither did Danny. I was hoping this whole "I found Jesus" thing would blow over after a couple of days and then everything would go back to normal.

But the exact opposite happened. Remember all those books Danny bought? He started reading them. And the Bible? He suddenly started reading that every day too. And for some reason, I would have a sixth sense when he would open it in the house. I'd be upstairs doing my makeup or something, *feel* the Bible open somewhere, and say loudly in a German accent, "Zare iz a Bible! And it iz open in zee house!"

Danny didn't go halfway; he went *all* the way with Jesus, and it freaked me out. Things between us got worse. When I would pick fights or be my usual snappy self, Danny fought back less and less. That irritated me too. It's not fun to fight with someone who doesn't fight back!

During this time, I started to formulate an exit strategy. I started calling old friends and people I used to party with, essentially going back to my old ways. God had come into our cozy, codependent abode and messed everything up.

Danny

It may seem odd that a guy like me, who grew up in a singing evangelist home, was now at a point later in life when he rededicates his life to Jesus. The difference was, at this new church, for the first time ever, I was learning about God's *grace*. In my early years, and on through college, my relationship with the Lord was performance-based, where I thought my right standing with God was dependent upon obeying all His laws, rather than on faith in Christ alone. I thought Christianity was all about perfectly following God's rules and regulations. And even though I saw God as being a good God, I still thought He was continually disappointed with me and my sinful ways. I knew I could trust God, but I thought that the degree to which He loved me and was willing to move in my life was based on my behavior.

Because of that belief, I never had any freedom or deep intimacy in my relationship with the Lord. I thought that every sin I committed, even the ones that would just pop into my mind out of nowhere, meant I was going straight to hell if I wasn't quick to repent every single time. So I ultimately had a roller-coaster relationship with God, feeling accepted one day and judged the next, which was just miserable. Every day, I walked this tightrope of religion, and it was exhausting. Sometimes I would make it across the rope and exhale in relief at the end of the day. But most days I would think or do something that I knew was displeasing to God and would fall off the rope again, into a pit of condemnation and shame. I felt like every Sunday at church I was going up to the altar to pray, and begging God for forgiveness. In my understanding, if I were to suddenly die, like being hit by a bus (at least, that's what I always envisioned), with any unresolved sin in my heart, regardless of whether or not my trust was in Jesus, then I was destined to spend eternity in hell.

With all of that wrong thinking I had about God, it's easy to see why attending this new church was so refreshing for me. For one, the transparency from the pulpit and church leadership brought a lot of hope. For the first time, I was experiencing a deep, personal relationship with God. That it's a relationship based not on what I do or don't do, but on accepting what He has *already* done for me. I was learning that it was less about religion and more about a relationship. All I had to do was receive by faith that the penalty for my sins—my sins of yesterday, today, and *forever*—was paid in full by the blood Jesus shed on the cross. This newfound freedom was so liberating that I wanted to share it with everyone, especially Kristin. I loved her, but I knew we couldn't continue operating the same way we had been and survive.

Even though I had this incredible revelation, I still had issues myself. Up to this point, I had been living a pretty selfish life. If you had met me back then, you probably would have said I was a "nice guy." Yes, I knew how to treat people, but at the end of the day, I was all about me. My reputation as a "nice guy" was due to the many great influences I had growing up, starting with my parents. Mom taught us about kindness, and Dad taught us about respect. Because of that, my selfishness wasn't always overt and in your face, but it was there. It would often come out in my irresponsibility and immaturity in certain situations, like not always being reliable or following through with things I said I would do, or even to the point of being careless with other people's hearts. Even now, self-ishness can still be a battle. Sometimes it's a daily fight not to serve my own interests but to look for ways to serve others. Thankfully, as I spend more time with God and read His Word, He is faithful to bring humility and self-awareness in these areas.

As Kristin and I continued to attend church every Sunday, and as I became more involved with the men's ministry, I saw other men living their lives in a way that inspired me to want to be better. Men who had healthy marriages, who were actively engaged in their children's lives, and who knew how to pray in faith. Men who knew how to fight—fight for their family, friends, and community. These were true leaders. These were *real* men.

At the same time, the better things became in my spiritual life, the worse things seemed to get with Kristin and me. My deep dive into all things Jesus really scared her. In codependent relationships, when one person makes a life-changing decision like this, the other person is often left wondering:

- What does this mean for me?
- What role do I play in all this?
- Does this require something from me?
- Do you need me anymore?

At the core, Kristin was scared that all this change in my life now meant she had lost control of things. And really, she had. That's the place God wants all of us in. He wants us each to have a heart posture that releases control and submits everything to Him, who is ultimately in control anyway. This fear led to intense pushback, often in the form of hurtful words. While I didn't, and still don't, always respond the way I should, I did my best to show her the love of Christ.

However, one of the major mistakes I made during this time was trying to get Kristin to see that life in Christ and with Christ is better. I tried so hard to convince her, in my own strength, that our future was with God. "Can't you *see* it, Kristin? It's going to be amazing!" I even asked if she could ever see herself singing Christian or inspirational music, to which she quickly replied, "Uh, no. I will *never* sing for Jesus." And I was like, "So you're saying there's a chance?"

If you've ever experienced a radical encounter with God before, then you know how strong the desire is to want the people closest to you to experience it as well. That was me with Kristin. But no matter what I said or did, everything seemed to push her further away, and things got worse before they got better.

For one, we agreed that the best decision was to move out and get separate places. Even though Kristin hadn't fully given her heart to Christ at this point, she still respected the pastor of the church we were attending, so we met with him about some of the problems we were having in our relationship. He didn't tell us to move out verbatim, but the gist of his advice was that we had some things out of order, and in his opinion, moving out would be beneficial. Surprisingly, we were both in agreement with his counsel and got separate places within a week or so of that meeting.

Moving out proved to be the right move (pun intended), but

The calm before the storm: out to eat in New York City on the infamous trip where we had a horrible fight and took separate flights home, 2007.

we still had major conflicts we couldn't resolve. Our crisis hit its peak on a trip we took to New York City. Kristin was doing some television hosting work at the Tribeca Film Festival, so we took advantage of the two weeks she had there to soak up some of the city together. We had dinner at the iconic restaurant, Rainbow Room, that sits high atop Rockefeller Center. During dinner, we had an argument, and as with many others, we just couldn't find any resolve. We left upset, which led to a long, tense elevator ride down sixty-five floors, followed by the two of us going in separate directions on the streets of NYC.

As I walked around aimlessly, God spoke to my heart and

made it clear that I needed to let Kristin go and let Him have her. He wanted me to trust Him with her completely. My head was so wrapped up in fixing our relationship that I couldn't see anything clearly. I was ultimately compromising my relationship with God and other people to cater to the needs of my relationship with Kristin. These were hard revelations because I loved K so much and was scared to let her go. I was scared that she would fall back into her old lifestyle and that there would be no chance for us to be together again. But, in spite of my fears, God made it abundantly clear that night that I needed to let her go.

Kristin

Things became so bad between us on that trip that we even took separate flights home. You know your relationship with someone is bad when you're willing to pay a change fee in order to not sit next to them. I remember calling Danny, nonstop, on the way to the airport. He wouldn't answer his phone. For someone who was extremely codependent at the time, this only made me more fearful, frustrated, and angry. The thought of sitting on a five-hour flight from NYC to LA without fixing things between us, even if it just meant putting a Band-Aid on things like we always did, drove me crazy. Obviously we'd had some pretty bad fights before, but this one felt different. I had always been able to get Danny to answer the phone eventually, but this time, the brother was done.

Danny

On the way to the airport, K kept making back-to-back calls and leaving angry voicemails. I found myself divulging all my drama to my taxi driver. Believe it or not, he gave me some much-needed advice by adamantly saying, *"Don't* answer that phone!" As simple as that sounds, it was profound to me in that moment. I had been so dependent on getting Kristin's approval that I usually would've answered the phone. But if I had, we likely would've eventually made up and then just continued the cycle of craziness. Well, not only did I *not* answer her phone calls, but when we got back to Los Angeles, I followed through by telling her that I was breaking up with her.

Kristin

I couldn't believe Danny actually broke up with me. He had tried many times before, but to no avail. I would always coerce him back into the relationship somehow. But this time he was sticking to his guns. I tried calling and left countless voicemails and text messages but heard nothing but crickets. And this was in 2007, back when sending a text message required extra time and tons of work. Remember those old-school flip phones that had the traditional telephone keypads with numbers that corresponded to letters? Yeah, those took some serious effort to get your message across. And there were no emojis to help you make your point. It was a nightmare!

So I did the only thing I knew to do. I went out and par-tied . . . every night. I called all my old friends, hit the bars and clubs, and numbed myself to avoid the pain my heart felt. Oh, but I was still going to church every Sunday—the same one Danny was going to. Except that now we sat on opposite sides of the sanctuary. Yeah, that wasn't awkward or anything, especially during the first few weeks, when the news of our breakup hadn't fully traveled yet. People kept saying, "Why are you sitting here? Didn't you see Danny? He's on the other side of the sanctuary. Do you want me to take you over to him?" Yeesh.

Danny

Our church had been promoting a women's conference that was coming up in the next few weeks, and God pressed it upon my heart to start praying in advance that Kristin would attend. I don't know why, but I just felt like He had something special in store for her there. But, at the time, a women's conference was the last place you would find Kristin. She wasn't comfortable in settings like that, mostly because she didn't feel like she had much in common with a bunch of Jesus-loving ladies. Regardless, I prayed that God would get her there somehow.

Kristin

The night of the women's conference, I had no intention of going. But that night, as I prepared to meet some friends for drinks, something made me change my plans. I now know it was God, but at the time, I didn't recognize that it was Him. I decided to quickly pop into the conference, wearing my single girl "night out on the town" clothes, and sit in the back so that I could leave early.

I had planned on staying through the worship music and then listening to the first few minutes of the sermon. This conference had several women scheduled to speak over the course of the next few days, and I had never heard of the woman speaking that night. As she started delivering her message, her story was eerily similar to mine in a number of ways. She continued, and it was like she was reading my mail. Oh, I was so annoyed with this woman right now! Because of her, I was already staying way longer than I had planned, and now she was making me *feel* things. She spoke with a strong Southern accent, which only added to her irritating charm. As much as I wanted to ignore everything that was happening inside my heart, I just couldn't. I stayed for the entire service, and at the end there was another one of those altar call thingies, where people are invited to come forward to receive Jesus into their hearts. Well, I, the one who thought, "I'm fine, thank you very much," went forward that night. The crazy thing is that I don't remember walking up to the front. It was like angelic hosts were ushering me—no, *pushing* me—to the front of the church. I was the first one to go up and the last one to leave. When I got there, I immediately knelt down with my face to the floor, so to this day, I have no idea if the altar was full, or if it was just me up there that night. But I didn't care. Finally, I had come to the end of myself, in complete surrender, and in that moment wanted nothing but Jesus.

When I left the church, the first person I wanted to call was Danny. I assumed he wouldn't answer, but I called anyway and planned to at least leave a voicemail telling him that I was sorry for everything.

Danny

That night when the phone rang and I saw that it was Kristin, my heart jumped. I had been watching the clock most of the night, praying that she had made it to the conference. During the past couple of months of our being apart, Kristin had attempted to make contact with me on several occasions, but I wouldn't answer any of her texts or calls. Not because I didn't want to, but because God had specifically told me not to. However, on this night, things felt different. I knew God was doing something. I answered the phone, and on the other end of the line was something coming from Kristin that I had never heard before: humility. In such a sweet and sincere voice, she explained how God had touched her heart and changed her life that night at the women's conference. She asked if we could meet up for coffee so that she could tell me all the details in person.

During our time apart, I had diligently prayed for Kristin every day. One of my friends from the men's ministry at our church at the time shared a Bible verse to help encourage me to keep praying. It was James 5:16: "The effective, fervent prayer of a righteous man avails much." One of the biggest things I learned during our breakup was the power of prayer—more specifically, the power of *fervent* prayer, of praying until God releases you from praying. Up until I had that revelation, I had worked tirelessly in my own strength to manufacture change in Kristin and my relationship. This approach not only ultimately failed, but it also left me discouraged and physically and emotionally exhausted.

Another verse that helped get me through this time, and that continues to be a key verse in our marriage when it comes to conflict resolution, is Ephesians 6:12: "We do not wrestle against flesh and blood, but against principalities, against powers, against the rulers of the darkness of this age, against spiritual hosts of wickedness in the heavenly places."

Our flesh, or our carnal nature, is easily offended and has an insatiable desire to be right. In relationships, when we fight with this "flesh on flesh" mentality, it's a recipe for drama and, ultimately, failure. Our greatest weapon against our flesh is prayer. Prayer is where we win the battle. Back then, and even now, I have to remember that my battle isn't with Kristin. It's with the Enemy and the powers of darkness that are relentless in their pursuit to split us apart. But no matter how dark or evil the plans against us are, the powers of darkness *have to* flee at the name of Jesus. I've seen it in my own life time and time again: the Enemy's greatest fear is a Christian who knows the power of the name of Jesus. So when I don't know what else to pray, just saying His name is enough to make the darkness tremble.

When we met for coffee, Kristin told me that she felt like God "reached down through a cloud of fears to rescue her" that night. She expressed sincere remorse and a pure desire to mend things between us. She gave a heartfelt apology, and I knew that God had performed a miracle.

Kristin

After the coffee meetup, we decided to get back together but to take things slow. It was as if we had two versions of our relationship, the prebreakup K&D and the postbreakup K&D. This time around we made some drastic changes in our relationship. We continued living in separate places, abstained from having sex, began praying and reading the Word together, and did our best to honor God with every aspect of our relationship. We both started serving in various ministries at church, and I even joined the praise and worship team and started "singing for Jesus," which I said I would *never* do!

My relationship with Christ didn't affect just my relationship with Danny, it impacted my professional life as well. The closer I drew to the Lord during this time, the less I desired some of the things I thought I had always wanted. For one, I turned down a three-year hosting contract with an entertainment network that I had auditioned for several times over the years. The offer was close to a million dollars and definitely would've taken my hosting career to a whole new level. But something strange happened. When the head of the network called to congratulate me, I found myself responding with, "Thank you so much for the opportunity, but would it be okay if I took the weekend to think about it before I accept the position?" My request surprised both of us, and he even chuckled a bit at the thought of someone needing to take a minute to think about this once-in-a-lifetime offer. Nonetheless, he obliged and gave me the weekend to consider the offer.

The truth is, I didn't need the weekend. I knew in my spirit that this job in particular wasn't the right place for me. Had the offer come a few years earlier, no doubt I would've jumped at the opportunity. But now the desires of my heart were shifting. The Bible says to "delight yourself also in the LORD, and He shall give you the desires of your heart" (Psalm 37:4). The more that I found my identity in Christ, the more my desires lined up with His will for my life.

Another big decision I made during this time was to quit the band I had been in for a few years. As my heart changed, the less I was able to authentically connect with the lyrics and overall creative direction of the group. Despite having cowritten nearly all the songs, I now felt detached from the words I was singing. Also, we played in various bars and clubs around LA, and being in those environments that once had such a pull on me no longer seemed like a wise choice. I tried to honor my commitment to the group, but it felt like I was living two different lives.

The band was scheduled to play at the famous Viper Room on Sunset Boulevard, and it would've been our biggest show to date. A&R reps from several record labels were planning to attend, my parents were going to fly in from Texas to see us play, and the guys in the band were counting down the days until the performance. But I knew this was no longer where God wanted me. So just two weeks before the show, I made the difficult decision to quit. The band members were devastated, and rightfully so. My parents were disappointed that they wouldn't be able to see me perform live. Of course, I felt horrible about letting other people down, but during that season, I learned that pleasing God will sometimes mean displeasing others. Not everyone will understand the Spirit-led decisions you make, but I encourage you to make them anyway. God will always work things together for your good if you trust Him and follow His lead.

In spite of the tough decisions I was making, at the same time, it was such an exciting time for both Danny and me. It felt amazing to start truly living a life of faith and trusting God with every decision we made. Even though we were living separately and had put new physical boundaries in place with each other, I felt more pursued and honored than in any other relationship I had ever had. The harder we both ran toward God, the closer we became to each other, and eventually, we started taking premarital classes at our church.

Danny: The classes were called "Helping You Say, 'I Do.'"

Kristin: When, in reality, it helped a lot of couples say, "I don't."

Danny: True. The classes definitely revealed some important issues between couples that may not have been addressed prior to the classes. The topics covered everything from the differences between men and women, communication, and finances to God's purpose for marriage. Unfortunately, a lot of times without classes like these, couples neglect talking about these areas prior to marriage.

Kristin: Yes, the classes were hugely beneficial for us. Between the classes and the amazing mentors God gave us during that time, we were set. All that was left for me to do was wait for you to ask me to marry you.

Danny: And waiting has never been one of your strong suits.

Kristin: Touché.

Danny: I had to get everything lined up first . . . like asking your Dad, getting the ring, and planning the perfect time and place.

Kristin: I'm so glad I waited, because your proposal was perfect.

CHAPTER 6

GOING TO THE CHAPEL

Danny

Even though it was evident that Kristin and I were headed in the direction of marriage, I still wanted the actual proposal to be a surprise. Kristin was scheduled to go to New York City for work, and I realized that her trip fell on the three-year anniversary of our first date. Even though we broke up for a couple of months, we still kept our original first date as the anniversary mark. I thought that would be a cool time to propose. Plus, given that our last trip to NYC had been a disaster, I wanted to redeem that city with an amazing memory. So from that point, I had roughly two months to pull everything together.

My grandmother had passed just a couple of months earlier, and I thought it would be special to keep her engagement and wedding rings in the family. I called my father and told him that I would love to propose to K on our dating anniversary and asked how he would feel about passing Grandma's rings down to me to give to K. He didn't hesitate. His eagerness may have had something to do with my being the youngest of three kids. My other two siblings were already well into their marriages and raising kids at that point, so I think my parents were more than ready to see me get hitched! He mailed the rings to me in California. That was another blessing that came from K and I now living in separate places—there was no chance of her getting the mail first and spoiling the surprise!

I asked K for her work itinerary so I could plan some fun things in the city for us to do in the pockets of time when she didn't have work commitments. I traveled with her on these types of trips often, so there was nothing out of the ordinary there. One of the first things I did was find out which hotel and part of town we would be staying in. Her work had us booked at a boutique hotel called 70 Park Avenue Hotel, in Midtown, right down the street from Grand Central Station.

I called the hotel in advance and told them what I was up to. The staff was all in on helping me pull off this surprise engagement. They went above and beyond. As I perused pictures of the hotel online, I saw that one of the rooms had a wraparound balcony and thought that would be an amazing place to propose, but wasn't certain I would be able to afford the room that came with it. So I left the reservation as it was and waited until we arrived to start making plans on the down-low while K was working. There were a lot of winks and "thumbs up" exchanged between me and the hotel staff. Since I had built some rapport with the employees, I knew they were doing their best to get us bumped to the penthouse suite, but I didn't find out for sure until the morning of the day I was planning to propose. They not only helped us switch rooms to the penthouse, but they did it at no additional cost.

Kristin

The network I worked for at the time was sending me to NYC to cover the red-carpet world premiere of *The Dark Knight*. Because this was one of the best superhero movies of all time, along with the tragic death of Heath Ledger just six months before the premiere, this event was one of the most massive red-carpet events I had the privilege of experiencing. The premiere was on July 14, 2008, the day before Danny and my official dating anniversary, which only added to the excitement of the trip.

The morning of the event, as we walked down the street to a quintessential breakfast diner in front of Grand Central Station, Danny got a call from one of the front desk ladies at our hotel. When he hung up and I asked him what the call was all about, he said something about how the hotel offered to upgrade our room for the troubles we had with the air-conditioning the night before. I remember being surprised because the air-conditioning thing was no big deal, and they had fixed it right away. Nonetheless, I said, "Really? Well, praise the Lord! Look at that favor!" Little did I know, Danny had been working tirelessly behind the scenes to upgrade us to the penthouse suite, but of course he couldn't let me know that, or I might have guessed he was up to something.

Once we returned to the hotel, we made our way up to our new digs. Our new room was, just, *wow!* The room itself was impeccable, but what made it over-the-top fabulous was the view. It was a corner room with a wraparound balcony, with incredible views of Grand Central Station on one side and the Empire State Building on the other. I felt like a princess. When I worked events like this, one of the perks was getting my hair and makeup professionally done, so that only added to the fairy-tale happenings that day.

After I got all dolled up, the plan was to go do my interviews with the cast on the red carpet and then head back to the hotel to pick up Danny for dinner. Everything was going swimmingly until I started to get a headache. See, I don't get just headaches. I get migraines. Often they can last up to twenty-four hours and may even involve vomiting. Fun times.

Despite the throbbing pain that was concentrated in my left eye (seriously, it felt like a tiny man was in my eye, hitting it repeatedly with a pickax), I did my best to make it through the interviews. The pain was so intense during the red-carpet event that I barely remember who all I spoke to that night. But I do remember that immediately after my interview with Christian Bale, I handed my microphone to my producer, ran all the way down the carpet behind a myriad of celebrities as they were doing their interviews with other media outlets, went behind the step-and-repeat banner, and vomited into a trash can—*at the world premiere of The Dark Knight*, in front of strangers, while wearing a fancy dress and trying not to mess up my professionally done makeup. If only I had a Bat-Signal to point toward the sky! Your girl needed rescuing. I mean, I still had interviews to do, plus dinner plans! Literally, the only thing separating me from hundreds of news cameras was a thin banner with Batman logos plastered across it. I've tried to look up media footage from that night to see if I can catch sight of myself full-on sprinting in high heels behind Christian Bale or Maggie Gyllenhaal but haven't had any luck. Please, do message me if you find something.

Danny

While I was back at the hotel prepping for the night ahead, I got a call from K's producer letting me know she had gotten sick from a migraine and wasn't doing well. After we hung up, I sent up the only Bat-Signal I had with me: prayer. "Lord, you didn't bring us this far for it all to not work out!" Everything up to this point had been playing out brilliantly, including supernatural favor from Him along the way. I prayed for healing for Kristin and that any of the Enemy's plans would be immediately stopped in Jesus's name. I was having a Holy Ghost moment up in that hotel room!

Kristin

I was still feeling awful as I rode in the taxi to the hotel. My eyes were supersensitive to any light, so I kept them closed the entire way. When I made it back to the hotel, I got onto the elevator to make my way up to our suite, but halfway up I started to feel sick again. I knew I couldn't make it to our room, so I got off on the next floor and frantically ran down the halls looking for a trash can. There were none to be found, so in a last-ditch effort, I opened a door marked "staff only" and threw up into a towel bin.

I eventually made it back to our room and flung myself face-first onto the bed. Danny was looking all dapper in a blazer, white button-down shirt, and slacks, ready to go to dinner and, unbeknownst to me, propose at the end of the evening. But at that point, the only thing I was ready to do was take a nap.

Danny

Back when I was researching dinner spots before we left for NYC, I knew I wanted to take K to eat somewhere in Brooklyn so that we could enjoy the view looking over the water, back at Manhattan. While researching restaurants, I came across a place called the

River Café, and it appeared to be the perfect romantic spot. So not only did we have a dinner reservation to get to, but our driver was downstairs waiting on us. Yes, I pulled out all the stops and ordered a car service that night! As K slept off her headache, I continued to pray that God would heal her. The engagement wheels were already in motion. We were here to redeem our time in NYC and to start a new chapter in our lives, and I was not about to let the Enemy steal this night away from us.

Kristin

After a forty-five minute nap, I miraculously started feeling better. I know it was God, on behalf of Danny's prayers, who healed me that night. Rarely do I recover from migraines that quickly, so I know the Lord was at work. I managed to freshen up within a few minutes, and off we went to dinner.

Danny

Our driver, Mike, drove us across the Brooklyn Bridge to the restaurant. Somehow, despite the migraine setback, we arrived early, so we went for a quick stroll down the Brooklyn boardwalk and took a few pictures with the Manhattan skyline as our backdrop. Then, after an amazing meal, we headed back toward the city. We had begun a nice rapport with Mike during the first leg of our trip, so conversation flowed all the way back to the hotel. We had a chance to share our dating testimony in detail with him, and as we spoke, the Holy Spirit's presence was evident. By the time we made it back to the hotel, we knew from the tears in Mike's eyes that the Lord had used our story to touch his heart, so we asked if it would be okay to pray for him. Right there, parked outside our hotel on the streets of NYC, we laid hands on Mike and prayed that the Lord would touch his life. It could not have been a more perfect way to walk into asking K to marry me. The Lord graciously gave me a glimpse of what was to come. Also, I was able to keep in touch with Mike for a couple of years after that, encouraging him in his walk with Christ.

Kristin

When we walked into the hotel room that night after dinner, I realized that Danny had plans beyond celebrating our three-year dating anniversary. With a little help from the hotel staff, candles were lit, one of our special songs was playing, and two chairs were set up on the balcony, with Danny's Bible on a table next to one of them. He led me out there, sat me down, and read Scripture to me, and we talked about our future together. Eventually, just one minute past midnight, on the official date of our dating anniversary, July 15, 2008, he got down on one knee and asked me to marry him. Spoiler alert: I said yes! Within a few minutes, champagne and strawberries arrived at our door. Oh, and Danny's grandma's rings fit me perfectly! I loved the thought of keeping these heirlooms in the family, and it only added to the perfection of the night . . . minus the migraine.

Danny

After the engagement was official, we stayed up extra late that night and called all of our close family and friends to tell them the news. We even started planning the wedding *that* night. Since we knew we wanted a fall wedding, we had to either act fast and pull one together in three months or wait a whole year. What do you think we chose? That's right, we rolled up our sleeves and went into game mode. We set a budget, planned everything ourselves, and started attacking the to-do list. We both agreed we were not going to stress about anything regarding wedding planning. We prayed about every detail, kept the main thing the main thing, and everything came together seamlessly.

Kristin

Well, *almost* seamlessly. There was the time when the flower guy called two nights before our wedding and *cancelled*. Like, "Sorry, but there will be no flowers at your wedding." After we had already paid a deposit and selected the arrangements and color schemes, he cancelled! And there was no time or money left to order from somewhere else. We didn't invest in any other decor, so flowers were kind of essential to bringing the whole wedding vibe to life. I'm grateful that we had been diligently praying about every detail and that God would keep us in His perfect peace throughout this process, because if it weren't for His supernatural grace, your girl would've had a bridezilla moment fo' sho!

As Danny spoke with the florist that night, we learned that this guy was going through a serious life crisis. Earlier that day, he told Danny, his wife had left him and, to add to his misery, had simultaneously closed all his business accounts. As Danny ministered to and encouraged him for almost three hours over the phone, we realized that God was giving us an opportunity to walk out our faith. We had prayed that our wedding would be less about the event and more about the covenant we were about to be under and the people who were going to be there to witness it all. In the grand scheme of things, not having flowers at our wedding paled in comparison to the grief, loss, and emptiness this man was experiencing. Peace quickly came to my heart, and I was prepared to move forward and have a wedding . . . sans flowers.

But God had other plans.

Danny

The morning of the wedding, while Kristin was at the hotel getting ready, I received a call from the florist. He expressed his gratitude for the time I had spent talking with him the night before and told me that he had managed to throw together some scraps from his shop and came up with enough floral arrangements to fill the tables at our reception. He even managed to bundle together some roses for the bridesmaids' and Kristin's bouquets. However, because he currently had no way to deliver them, I would have to find a way to pick up everything, *on our wedding day.*

I made it happen and arrived at the venue in time to put the flowers on all the tables. Friends and family collaborated to help pull everything together. One of our dear friends even brought a floral arrangement for the head table, and my sister-in-law plucked rose petals to disperse along the aisle where we would walk.

The only thing I wish we would've thought of and budgeted for is a day-of wedding coordinator. Because we didn't have one, the vendors were calling Kristin and me, asking all sorts of logistical questions as I was running around the venue. And Kristin was back in the hotel room with my mom, her mom, and bridesmaids, trying to get ready. I was talking to our pastors; greet-ing the photographers, videographers, and cupcake lady; helping the musicians; and fixing sound and speaker issues. Guests were beginning to arrive, so I found myself greeting them as well. I was literally breaking a sweat right up until I walked up to the altar.

Kristin

Our wedding day was such a test for me. I'm not a huge fan of surprises, and I like to be in control of as many things as possible. As we pulled into the venue, I had no idea what the flowers or anything looked like. I didn't know what my bouquet would look like, not even the type or color of the flowers. Would anything go together? Was there even a color scheme anymore? I had to release my tendency to try to fix things, and just go with the flow. That was hard but also an incredibly valuable teaching moment for me. God was showing me that "going with the flow" is a skill I was going to need to grow during this next chapter of my life. Being adaptable. Flexible. Open to change. Realizing that in life and in marriage, things won't always go as planned, despite our best efforts.

Before we got out of the car at the venue, as God was drop-ping all these thoughts into my spirit, my mom presented me with a ring of hers that I had adored from the time I was a little girl. It was a ring that her mom bought her back in her high school days. It was such a sweet moment, and I did my best not to cry off my freshly applied makeup. God was teaching me that some of the best things in life come when we least expect them and can touch our hearts and spirits in ways that "planned" things can't.

We walked into the room where my bridesmaids and I would

wait until it was our time to walk down the aisle, and I saw my wedding bouquet for the first time. It was an assortment of multicolored roses whose stems still needed to be evenly trimmed. We frantically looked around the room for anything that could neatly cut the stems, but all we could find was a dull knife in one of the drawers near the kitchen area. In a futile attempt to cut flower stems, minutes before we were to walk down the aisle, I had one of those laugh-cry moments—you know, where you somehow full-on laugh and full-on cry at the same time? It's like your body's way of releasing all emotions at once, a moment of complete surrender. To this day, it's one of the memories I treasure most.

My bouquet was far from perfect, but alas, the time had come. I linked arms with my dad and took the walk down the aisle that I had dreamed of since I was a little girl. Even though my dad is no longer on this earth and it pains me to think of all the moments he will miss with us here, I am so grateful that God allowed him to be here long enough to share that moment together. I didn't fully realize then just how much of a gift it was, but I sure do now. Treasure the moments, the big and the small ones. We aren't guaranteed tomorrow. Every day that you wake up with air in your lungs is truly a gift.

Danny and I were married outside, underneath a gorgeous, one-hundred-year-old oak tree trimmed with golden strands of twinkle lights. After Dad and I walked up the steps to the spot we were to stand, he kissed my cheek and then gave Danny a "good game" pat on his butt. The gesture caught us all by surprise, and the crowd of course loved it. It was Dad's unique way of giving me away but also a friendly reminder to Danny to treat me right, or else he'd *play*.

Our wedding day, October 24, 2008, at Calamigos Ranch in California. The one-hundred-year-old oak tree behind us, and Kristin holding the roughly trimmed bouquet.

We took a faith-filled leap into marriage that day. Little did we know that being married would require us to continue taking faith-filled leaps each and every day from that point forward. We once heard someone say that instead of saying, "I do," we should all say, "I have no clue." I don't know about you, but we for sure had no clue that day. No clue about what lay in store in the years to come. No clue that at the very moment we said, "I do," the Enemy was already plotting how to get us to constantly fight each other so that we'd be too distracted to fight him. And on the flip side, we also had no clue that in spite of our shortcomings and the Enemy's best efforts to mess things up, God already had wheels in motion to use every situation for our good and for His glory. Twelve years later, we are still in awe of how God successfully manages to redeem, reshape, and restore us *in spite of us*.

What the world calls "tying the knot" God calls "binding into one flesh." Danny and I were now two becoming one. We were trading our own ways for a better way. Not an easier way but a better one. A way that would require us to exchange our habit of self-reliance for dependency on God. A way that would hopefully allow our marriage to grow strong and last for a hundred years, just like that mighty oak.

We exchanged vows and rings and danced the night away.

Oh, and when it was all said and done, I couldn't have cared less about the flowers . . . or lack thereof.

CHAPTER 7

LAYING THE FOUNDATION

Kristin: In our vows to each other, I said you were "my best friend, my earthly rock, the love of my life" and that I was so honored to stand there with you. I expressed my excitement to go through life with you, fulfilling the vision God had given us. God knew we'd need it for the years ahead.

Danny: Absolutely. We promised to love each other even when it's hard and to do our best as a couple to reflect Christ. The commitment was to something much bigger than ourselves.

Kristin: We wanted to help each other be who God intended and to walk in the vision He had for us. And He graciously gave us many opportunities to uphold our vows in the first couple of years of our marriage.

Danny: True.

Kristin: Specifically, your promise that we would
be a team that reflects Christ. I tend to want
to fix things myself, but during our early
years, I learned the value of leaning into each
other's strengths and trusting God through
the changes.

Danny: I left my personal-training business and
took a full-time staff position at our church . . .

Kristin: and I had one of the busiest years of my
life working in television with jobs across the
country and abroad.

Danny: We tried to start a family—

Kristin: and lost our first baby during the first
trimester. We were told that it might take a
while to get pregnant again.

Danny: But within a month, we found out you
were pregnant with Harper.

Kristin: Because of all those experiences,
things like trust, teamwork, service, sacrifice,
forgiveness, and humility were all poured into
the foundation of our marriage early on. We
grew closer to the Lord and to each other,
even though we had no idea what was to
come in the years ahead.

Danny

The year leading up to our wedding, Kristin and I were basically full-time volunteers at our home church, so it was a natural

transition for us as a family when I accepted a staff position there just days after we were married. I had already felt God preparing me to make some type of shift into ministry like this, as many of my personal training sessions with a lot of my clients were turning into God-slash-therapy-slash-life-coaching type of talks. While I've always been and always will be passionate about physical fitness, I'm even more so when it comes to overall spiritual health and wellness. Even though I had a *good* thing going with running my own training business, the call to go on staff at our home church was the *right* thing. Often it's easy to let a good thing take the place of a right thing because the good thing is typically safer, more comfortable and predictable, and requires less sacrifice than the right thing. It was bittersweet to close my gym doors, but I knew in my spirit that it was time to trust God and take on this new chapter.

If you've ever been in traditional ministry, or know someone who has, then you know that when you go on staff at a church, while you may be hired for one role, ultimately you're signing up to serve wherever there is a need. Kind of like marriage, eh? At least, that's what my experience was like. I was hired to coordinate Sunday and Wednesday services and to lead the creative preaching team. But when I left the church staff three years later, I also led the men's ministry, oversaw the media department, launched a young adults ministry, and had my hands involved in nearly every outreach event. Any time the church doors were open, I was there. Oh, and K was too. They officially hired only me, but they got a twofer for sure!

Kristin helped me out in numerous ways, including delivering the church announcements at all three Sunday services every week, which essentially turned into comedy hour. We were definitely more effective in making people laugh than we were in relaying pertinent information to the congregation. For example, they may not have gotten all the correct details on the upcoming baptism service, but we sure got them laughing when we said, "If you're feeling funky, come get a dunky." We also worked closely together on the creative team; wrote, directed, and acted in many productions; and spearheaded the church's annual Helps Gala, a fun evening dedicated to celebrating our volunteers. Some of our closest friends in life and most-cherished memories came from serving in that ministry.

Looking back and recounting those early years of our marriage spent at the local church puts me in awe of God and just how much He loves and cares for us, even down to the most minute of details. Unbeknownst to us at the time, by delivering the announcements together, K and I got a small glimpse of our future, traveling to churches and corporate events all over the country, bringing love and laughter through our Date Night and Laughter Is the Best Medicine programs. By spearheading the volunteer gala each year, we learned what it takes to make a live event happen, from the planning to the people to the audio and visual components and everything in between. This was all a part of God's perfectly designed plan and His graciously preparing us for what we are doing now.

Reflecting back and seeing God's hand in our marriage, I'm amazed at how He supernaturally and carefully carved our story, knitted our hearts together, and helped us to lay a solid spiritual foundation during our early years. He knew we needed to build our love story on something more than just feelings. Feelings change. Feelings can lie. They can deceive and don't convey the full story. Feelings, important as they are, can anchor us in our own version of truth, rather than God's truth.

If we wanted a marriage that could go the distance, we needed something sure, steadfast, never-changing, faithful, and true. We needed a solid foundation. We needed Jesus.

Every other foundation is weak without Christ. A solid foundation is built on desperation for Him. See, we still need Him just as much today as we did back then. That desperation and longing to know Him more is a desire that, as followers of Christ, we all need to fervently guard, protect, and never let die.

During that season, as Danny mentioned, we spent a lot of our time at church. We took the verse "Those who are planted in the house of the Lord shall flourish in the courts of our God" (Psalm 92:13) literally. I experienced some of my busiest and most fruitful years as a television host during that time, so although most of my days were spent on set, filming for various projects, the second someone yelled, "That's a wrap!" I was in my car, headed for church to meet up with Danny.

Danny

Leading the creative preaching team, I helped bring the pastor's sermons to life, so to speak. Our team did a number of different things, from building a gigantic tomb for Easter Sunday to transforming our sanctuary into a football stadium for a Super Bowl Sunday illustration. We wrote original skits and vignettes to provide a visual presentation of our pastor's message. Our team was filled with incredibly gifted writers, directors, actors, welders, builders, and production coordinators. After all, this was Los Angeles!

We spent countless late nights at the church, creating sets and running rehearsals until the wee hours of the morning. Our team was composed of some of the most dedicated people on the planet. They not only were talented but also had a deep desire to know God and to make Him known. We opened every rehearsal with thirty minutes of prayer, solidifying the fact that we weren't just "doing theater" or putting on a fun little skit. We were putting the gospel on display, with the intent of reaching souls for Christ.

Before I came on staff, I served as a volunteer on this team. The man in charge was a guy who, in the years to come, along with his wife, would become a mentor of ours, and they have been instrumental in K's and my spiritual growth. I expressed my interest in joining the team, thinking I would fill any comedic acting roles that were available. Instead, he enthusiastically welcomed me onto the team and pointed up to the rafters of the church. "There's a spotlight that sits up there," he said. "We need you to turn it on and off a few times during service."

I did that mindless job for six months before ever stepping onto the stage for a production. Manning the spotlight was both humbling and formative in my spiritual walk. That role was humbling because after all those years spent growing up on stage in front of audiences with my family, there I was, alone in the rafters where no one could see me. And it was spiritually formative because it opened my eyes to the value of serving wherever there is a need. Jesus Himself came not to be served but to serve. He led with a servant's heart, always looking to meet the needs of others, and no job was too small.

You could almost say that K and I became addicted to serving at church. We loved working together and being a part of building something greater than ourselves. Whether I was operating the spotlight or was in the spotlight, we were blessed to be a part of productions that put the heart of God on display. As the altar was filled each Sunday with people receiving Jesus, we realized that no matter what area of the church we opted to serve, eternal fruit grew out of our service unto Him.

For me, during that season, God helped me to break the addiction of myself, or in other words, helped me to stop the "me first" mentality. I saw the freedom that came from taking the focus off me and putting the attention fully on Him. I no longer carried the weight of a performance, the success or the failure, on my shoulders. I became aware that any talent I may have is there solely because He graciously afforded it to me. And I began to hold everything with an open hand during that time, allowing God to give and take as He willed.

Kristin

After two years of Danny working on staff at church, I was about to give birth to our daughter, Harper. While we loved the time spent serving together at church, my television work had picked up as well, and with the new baby coming, we knew that something had to change with our busy work schedules. After much prayer, we decided that the best decision would be for Danny to leave his full-time staff position at church and move to a contracted, project-by-project basis to allow him to stay home with Harper when she arrived.

This decision proved to be one of the best decisions we've ever made. My work increased, and that year in particular, a lot of my jobs required me to travel across the country and abroad. Guess who got to come with me to almost every place I went? It was a mama's dream. I was able to continue working while having my husband and newborn baby at my side. The three of us went on roughly twenty trips that year, and we made incredible memories in places like New York City, Paris, and London. Just as I had fully supported Danny during his years on staff at church, he now fully supported me in my career. By coming with me on trips that required me to be gone for more than one night, he afforded me the blessing of not missing Harper grow up during her first year of life. I have to say, it was teamwork at its finest.

After about a year of life on the road, it was time to shift and make another family adjustment to help Danny fulfill one of his lifelong dreams. Remember the divine lesson that I learned as I cut my bouquet stems on our wedding day? The one about being adaptable and flexible? Welp, I was about to have yet another chance to sharpen those skills.

Danny

During my season spent on the road and at home with Harper, I utilized any extra time in my schedule to work on a dream I'd had since I was a kid: writing and performing a one-man comedy show.

Performing skits with my family throughout childhood cultivated my love of creating characters and making people laugh. My family's Christmas variety show ran for twenty years, and Kristin was even able to be a part of it before my parents retired. Beyond that, I was always looking for opportunities to practice my craft and perform throughout high school and college. For example, I spoofed the "church lady" sketch from *Saturday Night Live* at my high school talent show and, in college, performed a rendition of a "Spartan Cheerleader" from *SNL* at our annual college opening week festivities, "Ollies Follies." I've always felt at home on stage, so when I arrived in LA, one of the first things I did was enroll at the Groundlings, a well-known improv and sketch comedy theater.

After some time spent attending comedy school and hitting up open-mic nights around the city to test out my stand-up bits, once I recommitted myself to Christ, I quickly realized those environments may not be the best place for me to be regularly in and around, much as K started to feel about her band. The way most comedy clubs work, if you want any time to do your set on the main stage, unless you're a proven or well-known comic, you have to bring paying guests. By the time they paid for parking, a cover charge to get in, and a two-drink minimum, it was an expensive night just to hear my three- to five-minute set. Plus, they would often have to sit through several other comics whose material often wasn't as G-rated as mine, and it left me feeling a bit convicted.

It became clear that if I wanted to control not only the content but the environment as well, I needed to find my own venue to perform. So once I had a working script, including eighteen original characters and eleven wardrobe changes, I started my search for a theater.

It didn't take long. We found the perfect little black box theater available to rent that sat right along Ventura Boulevard, not too far from where we lived at the time. My one-man show had a name and a location; now all I needed was a ton of help. Unlike most one-man shows, mine took a multitude of people to pull it off. I had stagehands moving set pieces, a technical director managing lighting and sound cues, actor friends of mine who played small parts in a few of my sketches, a lobby crew taking tickets and showing people to their seats, and a three-person wardrobe team, headed up by Kristin, of course. My costume changes had to happen in under sixty seconds, and some were rather elaborate, like a cheerleader I played named "Honey" that required me to wear panty hose and press-on nails. There was no room for error, so we even had special rehearsals exclusively to go over the choreography and timing of my wardrobe changes.

Mario Barberio

Several of Danny's one-man show characters, 2014. From left: The Reverend, Grandma, Honey, Danny, MC Kevin, Toby Christopher, Arty.

Kristin

Nothing, *nothing*, tests the strength of your marriage more than the pressure of putting panty hose on your man in sixty seconds or less. Let's just say that I saw Danny in a whole new light. Well, we were backstage, so thankfully most of the time there was little to no light. But the scars are still there, nonetheless.

In all seriousness, the one-man-show experience brought Danny and me together in all kinds of new and interesting ways. Thankfully, most of them did *not* involve panty hose. We were both challenged and stretched, wearing many hats at once, from producing and directing, to coordinating rehearsals and casting, to designing and printing marketing materials like programs and banners, to overseeing the smallest details, like making sure there was someone greeting people at the door on show nights and preshow music playing in the lobby.

I loved seeing Danny do what he does best. He was built for the stage and to entertain live audiences. As confident as he is in his own skin, I think he may be even more confident when he is in character. It's truly a joy to watch.

Aside from watching Danny in his element, my favorite part was walking out onto the stage together after the show. We thanked people for coming and then asked if it would be okay to close in prayer. Every night, the entire crowd bowed their heads and joined us. It was powerful. To this day, it's how we end each one of our live events. And it's still my favorite part.

We ran Danny's one-man show for two Christmas seasons in LA, and shortly after the second run, I became pregnant with our son, Holt. He was born later that fall, and when he was just five weeks old, we decided that would be the perfect time to take him and Harper, who had just turned three, back to Indianapolis to run Danny's show for the Christmas season. That was a fun trip to pack for: car seats, strollers, all the baby things, winter wardrobe for four, and the additional luggage for Danny's wardrobe and all his props. Oh, and a snowstorm decided to arrive in Indy the same time we did. Good times.

The back-and-forth of supporting each other's dreams during those first few years proved to be crucial to the foundation we were laying. I was all in, supporting Danny when he went on staff at church. Then he was all in, supporting me and taking care of

Harper when my work picked up. And then I was all in, helping to bring his show to fruition. The unplanned ebb and flow of supporting each other was beautiful, and this commitment to positioning each other to shine hasn't stopped since.

God knew we were going to need every bit of what we learned during that season to prepare us for what He had planned next.

CHAPTER 8

FAITH CAN MAKE
YOU MOVE

Kristin: I can't believe it's already been over four
years since we moved across the country.

Danny: Yep. We left the beautiful palm trees
of Southern California for the glorious
cornfields of Indiana.

Kristin: Wait, remind me, why did we move
again?

Danny: (laughs) Well, it definitely wasn't *our*
idea.

Kristin: True. Even though it was a total "God-
thing," it was still tough.

Danny: Yes, by far one of the toughest decisions
we've ever made together as a family.

Kristin

Early on in our marriage, Danny began a tradition of getting away to the mountains for a couple of days every January to fast and pray, specifically for our family, business, and ministry. He prays more than once a year of course (haha), but this annual prayer and fasting getaway is of marked importance and has had a profound impact on our family throughout the years.

I call it his "Old Testament" getaway. He goes away to pray, to hear from God, and to gain vision and direction for the upcoming year. Then he comes down the mountain and tells the people (me and the kids) what he learned. We listen and obey for a few days, then, much like the Israelites, we rebel for the rest of the year, and then he has to go back to the mountain the following January to do it all over again.

Personally, I love when Danny goes away. Yeah, it's cool that he's "hearing from God" and everything, but y'all, I'm at home, *getting things done.* I don't know if it's because there is one less mouth to feed or what, but I always end up having oodles of extra time to myself, which I've learned that all married couples need in order to stay sane. Also, I'm an extremely competitive person who thrives on deadlines, so when Danny leaves for any set amount of time, it's like I'm suddenly in a competition with myself and the clock to bang out as many things as possible before he gets back. I'm painting something. Cleaning out drawers. Plucking my eyebrows. Taking long showers. Rearranging rooms. Watching a rom-com. Calling girlfriends to catch up. And, my favorite, sleeping in the middle of the bed!

Oh, and I also pray for Danny while he's away. Sheesh, I do have a soul. I'm not completely self-indulgent. The point is, his time away in the mountains is a blessed time for *both* of us. It gives me such peace and confidence as a wife to know that my husband, the spiritual head of our household, is choosing to make God a priority. And it frees up time in my schedule to tackle my to-do list, which is incredibly rewarding for my type A personality. It is truly a win-win.

Danny

One of my mentors inspired me to start the tradition of fasting and praying. Simply stated, biblical fasting is refraining from food for a spiritual purpose. Daily devotions are essential as well, but getting away from our normal routines to fast and pray often takes our relationship with the Lord to the next level. In Psalm 42 we see King David cry out to God during his time of prayer and fasting, longing to know and experience God in a more intimate and powerful way. If we want a deeper connection with the Lord, or in any of our relationships, quality time spent together is crucial for the overall health of the relationship. We make time for the things we care about. Jesus was intentional about getting away and spending time with His Father. If Jesus Himself chose to do it, how much more do *we* need it? Longer stretches of being saturated in God's presence, day and night, allows time for your flesh to become quiet so that the Holy Spirit can be heard.

The first year I started this tradition was January 2010. I took a list of things I was hoping to take to the Lord in prayer during my time away. I fully expected answers to everything on my list. Most of them were work related or personal things I was dealing with. But I quickly realized that this time alone with God wasn't about *my* agenda. It was about aligning myself with *His* agenda, being still, and hearing His voice. He sees our end from our beginning. He's all about the big picture. Yes, He cares about the details, but always with the end in mind. Once He reveals the vision, then He establishes His priorities in your heart. So I got to the mountain, set my list aside, and then left the mountain with a new list. Everything on God's list pertained to faith and marriage. I didn't know at the time that He was preparing my heart for what Kristin and I are doing in ministry now. The two subsequent years when I went to the mountain, He repeated the importance of our faith and unity in our marriage. That's how important faith and unity are to God. They bear repeating. God didn't allow me to move on to "my" list or anything else until I was faithful to commit to the directives He originally gave me.

Kristin

Back in 2013 Danny headed out for his yearly trip per usual. He had his overnight bag, Bible, journal, and an assortment of juices and soups. There is little to no cell service at the spot he stays, so it is a time for him to truly unplug and turn off the ambient noise so that God's voice can be amplified and heard clearly. In spite of my accomplishing a lot of menial tasks while he's away, I eagerly await for him to return from these trips because he always has something incredible to share.

That year in particular, I remember wondering what our "word of the year" would be. Peace? Joy? Shalom? Hopefully something feel-good and inspiring that I could have etched into a piece of wood to hang over the fireplace. At least, that's what I was hoping for.

After he walked through the door, rocking the handsome

scruff from not shaving for a couple of days and smelling of a man-in-the-woods type cologne, I eagerly asked, "How was your time away? Did God speak anything to your heart?"

"I have so much to share with you," Danny said. "But the big news is that I feel like He's telling me that we should move to Indiana."

To which I replied, "Uh, are you sure He's telling you to take *me* with you?"

He carried on about some other spiritual downloads that had supposedly occurred, but I don't remember anything he said after he dropped the we're-moving-across-the-country bomb on me. Move to Indiana? Has the man done lost his mind? Not once in the almost fifteen years that I knew Danny up to this point had we talked about moving to Indiana. This was not happening.

But, being the good Christian wife that I am, I politely said, "Well. Let me go pray and see if the Lord shall confirmeth these things that which you have saideth."

As I walked to the bedroom to pray, I began to tell the Lord what He should do. Basically, I was like, "God, you need to give me something super-spiritual sounding to confirm to Danny that this is *not* what we are supposed to do."

So I grabbed my journal and pen, sat on the bed, and waited for God to give me something. I couldn't believe the words that flowed: "Go, go, go. What's going to look like the end to a lot of people is going to be just the beginning of what I have in store for you and Danny."

Well, that's obviously not what I wanted to hear. But God doesn't always give us what we want. He gives us what we need, and this mandate was spot-on, whether I liked it or not. As some of my favorite Bible teachers say, "Let's unpack this passage."

First off, "Go, go, go" is crystal clear. God knows me so well. I need things to be made plain, so He gave it to me straight.

Secondly, "What's going to look like the end to a lot of people . . ." referenced that both of us would be leaving almost fifteen years of career experience and relationships in Los Angeles. For people who have careers in the entertainment industry, leaving the entertainment capital of the world for the corn capital of the world seems like a career-ending move.

Finally, "is going to be just the beginning of what I have in store for you and Danny" is the part of the mandate that requires faith, because it's filled with both so much promise and yet so many unknowns at the same time. For years, Danny saw us working in ministry together in some capacity. At one time, early in our dating relationship, the very word *ministry* made me feel sick to my stomach. I had a narrow mindset of what ministry meant and thought that particular profession was a call reserved for a handful of select people. You know, like Billy Graham and . . . okay, just Billy Graham. I thought that if Danny and I went down the ministry road, we would be pastoring a church or going door-to-door with salvation tracts, and both those options made me queasy.

So I came out of the bedroom and told Danny that he was right: God wants us to relocate to Indiana. We were excited for a few days, feeling like we had this new God-given direction and vision. We began making plans.

But then two years went by and we still hadn't packed one box.

You read that right. *Two* whole years. It took us two years to obey what God had clearly told us to do. Well, correction. It took *me* two years. Danny would've left California to start our new lives in Indiana the next day. Remember, he's the high-faith guy, and even if we were called to door-to-door ministry, that wouldn't frighten him. It would actually excite him. For me, because of the many unknowns and dots that still needed to be connected, I thought, "Hey, wisdom says to wait so God has more time to connect the dots. Let's do God a favor and postpone our move so that He can have more time to line things up perfectly before we go."

Also, every day, I would go outside and it would be 85 degrees and sunny, again. Getting smacked in the face with perfect weather every time you leave your house will have you quickly forgetting you ever heard from God. Why would God place those beautiful mountains and that magnificent ocean right there if He didn't want us to stay and enjoy His creation? That would seem like a blatant waste of His divine handiwork. What's the rush to move to Indiana? Let's just stay one more winter in California, and then we'll go. Also, why would God tell us to go somewhere without giving us a clear plan for jobs or without providing the specifics of how this was all going to work? That's so unlike Him, right?

Wait a minute . . .

Abraham.

Moses.

Noah.

Elijah.

Ruth.

Joseph.

The Israelites.

John the Baptist.

Paul.

Jesus . . .

Kristin and Danny.

The promise doesn't always come with provision at the start. Often provision comes as you *go*.

So after waiting two years to give God time to connect more dots, we knew less than if we had just gone when He told us to go in the first place. My television work in LA began to dry up, along with our finances. This was a self-inflicted wilderness we were experiencing. We weren't deliberately disobeying, but delayed obedience is still disobedience. It's like we tell our own kids: "Do what we asked right away, all the way." God told us to go, go, go, and instead, we stayed, stayed, stayed.

We needed the kind of obedience that Jesus spoke of when he said, "If you love me, you will obey" (John 14:15 GW). Ultimately, my hesitation to obey the Lord was rooted in a fear of failure and of what other people might think. If we moved because "God told us to" and then ended up failing, what would that say about God? What would it say about our faith?

The verse "faith without works is dead" (James 2:26) became uncomfortably real. We had the faith but lacked the action. Sincere faith should make you *move* . . . pun intended.

But here's how good and merciful God is. In the midst of our delayed obedience, He still continued to find ways to bless us. We may have not been in His perfect will at the time, yet He chose to love, teach, encourage, and strengthen us anyway. The lessons we learned during this time ended up being instrumental for our overall spiritual growth and fortitude. One blessing that stands out the most is when a couple at our home church, whom we didn't know well, came up to us after service one Sunday, handed us a check for $1,000, and told us specifically that they wanted to "sow into our ministry." You know—the "ministry" we didn't even have at the time? The word that used to make me queasy? Yeah, they were sowing into that.

This couple had no idea that God had told us to move to

Indiana and that we had been dragging our feet for two years. And none of us had any idea that in just one year's time, we would be running a full-fledged ministry both online and in-person through live events. But God knew, and in the midst of my hesitation to follow God's lead, He graciously used the faith and obedience of another couple to bless and encourage us. That's when I learned firsthand that obeying God isn't just about getting blessed. God always has someone else in mind on the other side of our obedience. In the kingdom of God, obedience is often about someone else. The ripple effect of obedience is eternal, and that's why He cares so much about it.

After this experience, we're convinced that most of the time, it's not that we need more faith. Jesus said that all we need is faith the size of a mustard seed. That's not very much. So, no, it's not that we need more faith. We need more obedience. We need to put our faith into action and *do* the thing that we already know to be true in our heart.

Danny

Have you ever felt as if the Lord was asking you to do something big? Something that would drastically shake and shift things in your life? The call is so powerful, you can practically taste it. You get so pumped as you envision yourself doing it, and you're like, "Let's go!" But after you take a few steps and start realizing all it will take to actually pull it off, you start pumping the brakes. Then you start questioning everything. "Where do I start? How do I fund this? Who will help me? Am I qualified? Am I smart enough? Do I really have what it takes?" Before you know it, you find yourself laying down the dream and slowly walking away.

But after that, every time you find yourself in the presence of the Lord, that call comes back. Deep calls unto deep, faith rises up, and you know that you know you should be doing the thing God asked you to do. Then all the question marks and what-ifs enter your mind, and you avoid your assignment yet again. This happens over and over to the point where you find yourself with a huge, unsettled place in your soul, but in spite of that, you feel like the moment has passed you by and it's too late.

Well, we want to encourage you today that it's not too late to pursue what God has called you to do. If God has called you to it, nothing can successfully stand against you. He equips those he calls with everything they need.

And ultimately, when God has something for us to do, it's never really just about us. He always has someone else in mind on the other side of our obedience. So if it's not about us anyway, why not just get out of the way, start walking in obedience by faith, and see all that God has in store? And if you feel that your time has passed, know that God is the redeemer of time! He works outside of time and space and can suddenly put things into place in His perfect timing.

That said, embrace and enjoy the process of whatever He has called you to accomplish in the meantime, because that's part of how you grow and mature in the journey. It's also the preparation you will need to sustain victory once you've reached the goal.

Kristin

So, finally, we put a date on the calendar to move to Indiana. It looked like an abrupt decision to almost everyone in our lives, but again, we were two years late for an appointment, and now we were in a rush to get there!

Our last Sunday in California was one of the hardest days we've ever experienced. That was the day we officially said good-bye to our church family. We had done so much life and been through a lot with these amazing people. At the end of the service, we were asked to come up to the front of the sanctuary so that the pastor and leadership team could pray for us. As we stood up there with our heads bowed, alongside our two kids who were ages five and two at the time, the entire congregation stretched out their hands toward us as the pastor prayed. I remember my tears welling up, eventually pouring out and hitting the floor beneath me. The mix of emotions I felt—sadness, gratitude, love, grief, and peace, all at the same time—was coming out of me in the way of buckets of tears.

Toward the end of his prayer, the pastor asked the leadership team to place offering buckets up front and then invited forward anyone in the congregation who felt led to bless us financially to help with our cross-country move. Oh my. I had seen this done in church before, but for *other* people. Now that it was *us* standing up there, I was so uncomfortable. I wanted to be the one in a position to bless others, not the one who needed the blessing. As people got out of their seats and made their way forward, I couldn't even look up to see their faces. It was all so humbling and overwhelming.

Before we went home that day, the treasurer handed us a check for the amount that people had placed into the offering buckets. When we opened it in the car, I nearly fainted. It was within pennies of the total amount that our moving truck cost!

Danny: Before we knew it, it was time to pack up our entire home.

Kristin: We had a massive packing day the day before we left, when about ten families from our church came over to help us load the truck. There were dollies with appliances

Standing on our Tetris-packed moving truck, preparing to say goodbye to California and hello to Indiana, 2016.

rolling this way and that, teams of two carrying large pieces of furniture here and there, and people cleaning and throwing things into the infamous box marked "miscellaneous."

Danny: We had a lot of laughs, shed a lot of tears, and hugged a lot of necks that day. I don't think the last family left until close to one o'clock in the morning. Then the four of us slept in an empty house, on a lone mattress in the living room. Such a sweet memory.

Kristin: The next morning you got the kids and me off to the airport for our direct flight to Indianapolis, while you hung back to get last-minute things loaded onto the truck and to meet the person driving the truck for us.

Danny: Right. And I hopped on a later flight with our cat, Odie, my little furball flying buddy.

Kristin: I got the kids; you got the cat.

Danny: Speaking of the cat, on the way to the airport, he was so nervous that he clawed his way through his carrying case. I had to make an emergency stop at Home Depot to grab some zip ties to make it secure enough for the flight. Needless to say, we barely made the flight that day.

Kristin: Well, at least you were with Odie. He always landed on his feet.

Do you need to "move"? It could be a physical move like ours was, or maybe it's a spiritual shift in an area of your life God wants to address. Here's how Danny has sought clarity:

Danny's Old-Testament Getaway Checklist

- ☐ Set a date on the calendar for your prayer and fasting retreat. Plan to be gone for a minimum of twenty-four hours and up to seventy-two if you can. The location should be as simple as possible: anywhere that has minimal distraction. Grab a tent and go camping if that's your thing, or see if there is someone in your network of friends who has a guest house or second home they will allow you to use.
- ☐ If you're not already reading the Bible daily, do your best to start before you go on the getaway. It will prepare your heart and put you in a place to discern God's voice clearly.
- ☐ Make a list of the things you need clarity on, but once you make it, hold it lightly. God may flip the script and address things you weren't even aware needed attention.
- ☐ Think about what kind of fast you can commit to. The Daniel Fast is one of our favorites, which consists of eating vegetables, fruits, nuts, and legumes and drinking water, herbal tea, or freshly squeezed juice. You can even have coffee! Just omit the cream and sugar.
- ☐ Pack your food and drinks, Bible, journal, a pen or pencil, and a worship playlist. I also like to bring a couple of books on topics that I'm looking to grow in, like leadership, marriage, and so on.
- ☐ Go alone. This isn't the time to bring a buddy.

☐ Start your mornings with worship music and a hike or something active. It gets your blood flowing and puts you in a place of praise and adoration.

☐ Spend time throughout the day meditating on God's Word, praying (out loud), and listening to what the Holy Spirit says.

☐ Journal and write things down as much as you can while you're away.

☐ Most importantly, aim to *enjoy* your time with God.

☐ When your time away is over, don't forget what God revealed to you. It's easy to forget once you "come down from the mountain."

CHAPTER 9

HELLO, INDIANA

Kristin: We finally made it to Indiana. Better late than never, right?

Danny: Right. We packed up our 1950s matchbox home in California in less than thirty days, sold a car, gave away a car, and headed across the country with two kids and a cat.

Kristin: And we rented a home, sight unseen. That was for sure one of the craziest things we've ever done.

Danny: We were smart enough to send a family member over there to make sure it was a legit rental and that we weren't getting scammed or walking into some type of squatter situation.

Kristin: Thankfully, it ended up being the perfect place. Everything seemed to be lining up beautifully. The move went as well as a move could go, and we found a great neighborhood

and home. Except one minor detail was still
hanging in the balance.

Danny: What's that?

Kristin: Money. How were we going to make
money?

Danny: Oh yeah . . . that.

Kristin

Once we arrived in Indiana, I think I expected there to be a gigantic box labeled "Blessings" waiting on our front doorstep, some type of instant reward from God for obeying His command, even if we were two years late. But, unfortunately, that's not quite how things unfolded.

The only clear mandate we had was that we were to start making "family-friendly videos where God is always welcome." We didn't have any fancy equipment, and we were just getting our feet wet with our social media presence. We were filming with our trusty iPhones, and Danny had taken some editing classes at our local Apple store before we left Los Angeles. Now we just needed to start filming something. Before we left LA, we posted a couple of lip sync videos and some other fun, sporadic, light-hearted content that seemed to resonate with our audience. And by "audience," I mean mainly our families, close friends, and Danny's parent's local church in Brownsburg, Indiana. It was a small but mighty fan base, and the early response was strong enough to encourage us to keep going.

Once we officially had boots on the ground in Indiana, we committed to posting one video each week. Even though we had no idea how we were going to monetize our content, we knew, at the very least, that we had to be consistent with our posts. It was an exhausting yet exhilaratingly creative season for both Danny and me. We have such fond memories of that first year in Indiana, putting the kids to bed, throwing on a pot of coffee around nine o'clock, and sitting around the kitchen table brainstorming and planning our weekly video.

Despite all the creative fun we were having and the encouraging responses we received after every video post, the fact of the matter was that no money was coming in, and I'm the type of person who needs to see an instant return on investment, or I'm out. Our influence was increasing, but our bank account was decreasing. To "walk by faith, not by sight" (2 Corinthians 5:7) is challenging when what you see is imminent debt. The emotional high that the success of our videos gave me was cut short by the surmounting fear and uncertainty that came with our bills that were quickly piling up.

Contrary to popular belief, viral videos don't always translate to dollar bills. If we had a nickel for every video view we had at that point in time, we would be millionaires. But instead, the exact opposite effect was happening. The more social capital we built, the less actual capital we had. I found myself doubting not only our entire cross-country move but all of our life choices up until this point. That's the thing about worry and doubt. If you give them an inch, they'll take a mile. Prior to this challenging time, I would have described myself as someone who had faith that God would provide, but it's easy to say you have faith in something until you actually need that something. Faith for finances? Yes, and amen . . . when our bank accounts were healthy and strong. But now that the safety net of a weekly paycheck was removed and we were essentially starting our own business and living off our savings for the unforeseeable future, what little faith I did have quickly gave way to fear.

During this season, Danny couldn't keep up with my mood swings. I'd be jumping for joy one minute and curled up in a corner, bawling my eyes out, the next. Danny is more—what's the word? Stable. That's it. Since I've known him, circumstances have never seemed to affect his faith. He's the "best-case scenario" king, and I'm the "worse-case scenario" queen. We could be down to pennies in our bank account, and Danny "Hakuna Matata" Adams would be all smiles, knowing that someday God would use our testimony of lack and hardship to bless other people. He takes the "all we need is Jesus" thing literally. Me? I'm over here preparing for the house and cars to be taken away, imagining us shuffling along the side of the road in our bathrobes, with no money, no plan, or hope for the future.

I'm of course grateful to have a husband who is full of faith. But in those frantic moments when I just wanted someone to match my mood and validate my feelings, Danny's faith would often irritate me. In the middle of my nervous breakdown, he would suggest that we pray, and that suggestion would make my head spin. No, I don't want to pray! I want to freak out and eat an entire chocolate bar on my own right now, thank you very much.

Danny

K and I handle crises very differently. After knowing Kristin for as long as I have, I've learned that, for her, timing is everything. I now know I shouldn't offer prayer *during* a nervous breakdown or *before* she has her candy bar. She needs to get all the feelings out, and then she's typically in a better place to receive advice or suggestions from me afterward. And while she appreciates the prayer, she would much rather have me match her emotions and enjoy some chocolate alongside her first.

On the flip side, just as my seeming lack of worry often bothers Kristin, her seeming lack of faith often bothers me. It's something we are continuing to work on understanding more in each other, and one of the many ways that God has used the strength in one of us to help cover or carry the weakness in the other.

For as long as I can remember, having faith that things will work out has always come naturally to me. I'm an eternal optimist and always believe for the best, both in situations and in people. I grew up in a Christian home where trusting God was second nature. We didn't have a lot in the way of material things, but we were rich in faith. I always figured that if I have enough faith to trust God for my eternal salvation, then why wouldn't I trust Him with everything in my life on this side of heaven?

When I was growing up, my family attended a modest church that was full of sweet people ready to testify of God's faithfulness every Sunday morning. At one point in the service, the preacher would give time for people to give personal testimonies, or, as our church liked to call them, "popcorn testimonies." This is when someone in the congregation would stand up and give a short praise report on something God had done in their life that week. This would lead to another person standing up to testify, and so on and so forth. Because of these testimonies, I was able to witness firsthand God's faithfulness in the lives of His people on a regular basis.

In my own life, when trials and troubles come, I may be down or bummed for a while, but I've never been one to stay in that place for long. I've learned that it's better to be led by my faith in Christ, who never changes, rather than my feelings, which can always change. Our former pastor used to say, "Just walk by faith, and your feelings will catch up."

Kristin

One of the lowest points I can remember during our first year of living in Indianapolis was the time we had nearly depleted all of our savings and could barely afford groceries for the week. For years we had a large, clear water jug that Danny decorated back when we were dating. The idea was that we would put all our loose change in there to save up for a trip overseas. He made sweet little hand-drawn signs that read "Prague" and "Budapest," two of the cities we dreamed of going to together someday. We had already saved up enough to take a trip to Eastern Europe, and now we were filling the jug for a second time. Because our savings were running out, and I was determined not to take another early withdrawal from our 401(k), it became apparent that we were going to have to use the water jug coins to buy groceries.

To say this was a humbling experience is a drastic understatement. I was so full of pride and embarrassed to admit that we were in such dire financial straits. Nonetheless, I swallowed my pride and lugged that ginormous jug into the grocery store and headed straight for the coin-counting machine. My stomach was in knots, and I felt miserable inside, but I did my best to smile and put on a happy face for the kids. Harper and Holt were five and three years old at the time, and they of course had no idea that we were struggling to make ends meet. They not only were oblivious, but it turns out that they *love* coin-counting machines!

They had the time of their lives pouring the coins onto the metal ramp and watching the machine sift them through.

While the kids were enjoying themselves, I was struggling to hold back the tears. Then suddenly, Harper said, "Mom, look!"

She grabbed what looked like a special, shiny coin of sorts and held it up for me to see. But it wasn't a coin . . . it was Danny's wedding ring! He had lost it several months prior, and honestly, we were resigned to the fact that we were probably never going to find it. All the while, it had been lying hidden in the vacation jug, mixed in with all the coins.

I quickly realized how this must have happened. Danny always takes off his wedding ring when he goes to the gym, and occasionally puts it into his pocket. Then when he comes home, he throws any loose change he has into the vacation jug. Evidently, one day he must have grabbed what he thought was just a pocketful of coins, but also included the ring, and thrown them into the jug.

Our coin-saving jar that we were planning to use for a trip overseas until we needed it to buy groceries when our finances were running low. It's also where Kristin and the kids found Danny's lost wedding ring.

I often wonder why God doesn't answer our prayers when we want them answered. We had prayed to find that ring several times to no avail. But the thing is, His thoughts are higher than our thoughts. His perspective is higher than our perspective. Often when it may seem as if God is withholding something *from* us, He is actually trying to get something *to* us.

I didn't know I would one day be standing side by side with my two small children in front of a coin-counting machine as our last resort, but God did. And He decided for that to be the moment for us to find Danny's ring. Why? I can only speculate, but I think God was symbolically reminding me of His faithfulness. That wedding ring is a symbol of a covenant, an unbreakable promise between two people. Just as Danny and I are under a covenant together, we are under an even greater covenant with God. In that moment, just when I needed it most, I was reminded that God never breaks His promises. His word is a sure thing. If He said it, then it is so!

I stood there at the coin machine, holding the wedding ring, and began to laugh-cry, as I did with the flower stems. When you full-on laugh, full-on cry at the same time, you may look hysterical or mad, but in spite of that, it's one of the most freeing things I've ever experienced. It's happened only a few times in my life, but when it does, it usually signifies that some type of significant or spiritual breakthrough has occurred for me. In that moment, even though our financial circumstance hadn't changed, my mindset had. I knew that God had not forgotten about us and that somehow everything was going to be okay.

Just a few weeks after Kristin and the kids found my wedding ring, I received a call from a pastor out of Oklahoma City. He said he and his wife loved our videos and that they really appreciated the type of content we were creating. He went on to say that his church had a marriage conference coming up in a few months and asked if we would be interested in ministering. First, he wisely confirmed that we were in fact Christians. Then he went on to say that he could easily bring in a pastor friend of his to help lead the conference, but he believed that God was calling him to think outside the box and do something different—in this case, with us involved, *way* different. This pastor was either out of his mind or led by the Holy Spirit. Turns out, he was both! Sometimes you have to be out of your mind so that you don't lean on your own thoughts or understanding.

I told him that while I had known for a long time—twelve years, to be exact—that Kristin and I would ultimately be in some type of ministry together, this would in fact be our first time leading a marriage conference. We had attended a lot of marriage conferences, not because we were one of the speakers but because we desperately needed help ourselves. I told him that if he was comfortable with having us, given that we had no ministry track record, we would be honored to come and share our story with his congregation.

He told us not to worry and that he would have our backs if we needed saving. We figured, hey, he's the one taking a risk on some lip sync folks from the internet, so this is on him if we crash and burn! But in all seriousness, we knew this opportunity was a God thing. At this point in time, we had not marketed or promoted ourselves as speakers, yet in spite of that, we were being booked to speak at our first marriage conference.

Somehow, in less than a few months, we needed to put together enough speaking material to fill four hours on a Saturday, plus three Sunday services as well. The conference was scheduled for Valentine's weekend 2017. To give a timeline, we relocated to Indiana in May 2016, the coin-machine-wedding-ring incident happened that October, and the following month, we got our first call to speak at an event.

Of course, neither of us felt ready or qualified. But thankfully, God doesn't always look for the most skilled and knowledgeable person to accomplish His purposes. He simply looks for those who make themselves available and who will stand with Him by faith. So that's what we did.

In addition to keeping up with our weekly videos and homeschooling the kids, we set aside some time to write and put together our conference topics and sessions. And then, a few weeks before the conference, the water went out in our home . . . at the end of January . . . in the middle of winter in Indianapolis. Fun times. Apparently there was an issue with the pipes, and it was going to take a week or so to fix. During that time, our next-door neighbors graciously offered us their place so we could shower. This sweet family already had eight children of their own; they definitely didn't need four more people coming over every day to use up the hot water! We would bundle up, walk next door, and then head back to our place with wet hair in below freezing temperatures. It's no surprise that within a few days, all four of us got sick. To top things off, because of the nasty cough that came with the sinus infection I was battling, I completely lost my voice for the entire week prior to the conference.

Needless to say, our plans to organize and finalize our conference content went out the window. Also, our financial situation still hadn't changed, so there was that added pressure as well. Nonetheless, we pushed through and eventually boarded the flight to Oklahoma City. We were flying on a hope and prayer for God to get us through this weekend.

Prior to our getting sick, we had filmed a lip sync video that I was in the middle of editing. We left for OKC on a Friday morning, and our goal was for me to finish editing it on the first leg to Chicago while Kristin attempted to formulate our speaking notes into some type of game plan.

We landed in Chicago only to find out that our connecting flight was delayed, so we thought we would make the most of the time and, at the very least, get our video posted. We grabbed some water, found a spot to set up my computer and make progress on Kristin's notes, and got back to work. When I opened my computer to export the video out of my editing software, the video was nowhere to be found. Somehow it had disappeared from my editing timeline. I've had technical issues with our computer before, but nothing like this. It was truly bizarre.

The lip sync videos we make are a ton of fun but require a lot of work. We have anywhere from fifteen to twenty costume changes each (plus makeup changes for Kristin), and in addition to taking several days to prep and several days to film, it then takes me several more days to edit the clips together. So this missing video meant a couple of weeks' worth of work was potentially wasted.

I quickly jumped on the phone with technical support, who did their best to troubleshoot for a couple of hours, only to find out nothing. Then, during my call, Kristin accidentally spilled our drinks all over her journals and papers with our notes for the conference, so now the few plans we did have were covered with water stains.

Kristin, who we all now know tends to freak out in situations like this, handled the crisis like a champ. With what little voice I had left, I turned to her and said, "I'm not exactly sure what God is up to, but I know He's up to something." He wouldn't have brought us this far only to watch us fail. These unfortunate things that were happening to us were clearly spiritual attacks designed to discourage us, to weaken us, and ultimately, to get us to abort the mission. Well, not today, Satan. We packed up our things, boarded our connecting flight, and kept our eyes fixed on Jesus.

Just because we kept our eyes on Him didn't mean things got easier. We found ourselves in the back row of a small shuttle plane, with severe turbulence almost the entire way from Chicago to OKC. While Kristin did her best to read the smeared ink from the wet notes and transfer them onto some airplane napkins (the only "paper" we had available), I was busy trying to manage a major headache, which, by the way, I never get. I think I can probably count on both hands how many times I've had a headache throughout my life. The Enemy was definitely trying to derail what was about to happen over the next couple of days.

Once we landed in OKC, we headed to baggage claim only to find out that our luggage was missing. Seriously? Now, this is just plain comedy. Thankfully, after a couple of hours, it arrived on another flight, close to midnight. In less than nine hours, we were scheduled to start speaking in front of over two hundred people. At least Kristin was, because I still had little to no voice.

We made it to the hotel, grabbed a few hours of sleep, and woke up at six o'clock. I was gargling salt water, drinking hot tea, and praying nonstop. When we arrived at the church, the media team asked if we had any slides, Scriptures, videos, images, PowerPoint, and so on to help with our presentation—you know, like most professional speakers would typically have with them.

Almost in unison, we ashamedly replied, "Uh, no. No, we don't." As couples filed into the sanctuary and took their seats, Kristin and I found a quiet place to pray. Now, before you start envying how spiritual we are, you should know that our prayer went something like this: "Well, Lord. It's only You that could've gotten us this far. . . . Now what? Crap. Amen."

And then we sat down, trusty airplane napkin notes in hand, waiting for the pastor to introduce us. Sink or swim, here we go!

We took the stage, and as we started sharing our story, I remember a supernatural peace immediately coming over both of us. All the setbacks we had just gone through in the weeks leading up to the conference made this moment that much sweeter. I'm sure our words didn't come out perfectly or just right, but they sure did flow, which was a miracle in and of itself, since minutes before, I barely had any voice at all. We hadn't rehearsed or practiced anything. Our only plan for the first session was to

Acting like we were prepared and knew what we were talking about at our very first marriage conference at Faith Church in Oklahoma City, 2017.

tell them a little about us, as well as our dating and marriage testimony. Kristin had a couple of bullet points and stories she was planning to share, and I had the same. We did our best to stay in sync with the Holy Spirit and piggyback off each other's words.

Luke 12:12 (The Voice) says, "The Holy Spirit will give you the words to say at the moment when you need them." We know this was the case that day, because during that session, Kristin said things I'd never heard her say before, and I said things I'd never said before. We weren't completely sure how the audience was receiving our message, but *we* were sure blessed by the words that were coming out of our mouths! (haha) But seriously, any good that came from our sessions was not by our doing but all because of God's grace. It was one of the most incredible supernatural experiences we've had to this day. To make things even better, the view we had from the stage was the *exact* snapshot God had given me back when Kristin and I were dating. This, right here—Kristin and I doing ministry together—was the fulfillment of a twelve-year promise that God had put in my heart. This realization was overwhelming, and I cried like a baby as I told the story from the stage.

We had about fifteen minutes to connect and regroup between sessions, and after the first one, we were beside ourselves and in awe of what God just did. We had two more sessions to go, and God faithfully continued to show up and lead us throughout the day.

After the conference we grabbed a bite to eat with the pastors and then headed back to the hotel to prep for the next day's Sunday services. Before we started prepping, Danny checked his computer to see if there was any change in the status of our missing video. To our surprise, some of the footage seemed to be back in place, so he thought he would give technical support another try. After a few hours of troubleshooting, they were able to recover most of the video! The editing technician patiently helped Danny piece it back together, clip by clip, and we now had roughly 80 percent of everything restored. It was like the cherry on top after an already incredible day. Thank you, Jesus!

Earlier that evening during dinner with the pastors, we shared about the spiritual attacks we had prior to the conference, so they knew all about our missing video. When the pastor learned that we were able to recover it, he immediately decided that the "world premiere," as he called it, of our latest lip sync would be at the top of each Sunday service as part of our introduction.

The next day we sat with a live audience as our "Love Songs of the Decades" lip sync played. For the first time, we were watching something that we created together along with a live crowd. Up to this point, we clicked Upload and hoped our videos would bring joy to some people. Now we were able to witness firsthand the impact our videos were having. Seeing and hearing people smiling and laughing at our antics was such a gift, one I'll never forget. It was like a huge hug from heaven.

By the grace of God, we made it through all three services. Our sermon was based on our move from California to Indiana and included much of what we shared in the previous chapter on the topics of faith and obedience. It was so cool how God set up everything for us to use our cross-country move as a sermon illustration, because that particular church where we spoke was about to move into a new building after many years at their current location. God is in the details, y'all. He cares about everything that concerns us. Even when you can't see or feel Him, He is working all things together for your good!

We said goodbye to our new church family in OKC and headed back to Indianapolis. Danny put the final touches on our lip sync video during the flight, and we finally posted it before we went to bed, close to one o'clock in the morning.

When we woke up, we checked our Facebook page to see how the video was doing. I thought something was wrong with my phone or our Facebook account because it said we had over one million views and that it was being rapidly shared by the second! Within twenty-four hours, we surpassed five million views, and when it was all said and done, nearly thirty million views. What took things over the top was when other large platforms asked us if they could natively share our videos to their pages. We agreed, and then the video went viral on their pages as well. At one point we added up the combined views from all the different pages that shared it, and it was over three hundred million! We had a couple of videos go viral prior to this, but none of them came close to the international reach this had. People from all over the world commented on the video, from Australia to South America, from England to Canada. And our number of followers jumped from sixty thousand to five hundred thousand that week alone. The Book Now button on our Facebook page was clicked fifteen thousand times over the course of the next two weeks, and we received well over a hundred official requests to come and speak or entertain at churches, corporations, and charity events.

With all the excitement and updates coming in during that time, we barely got any sleep. We were even invited to come and share our "viral video" story on a local morning news program here in Indianapolis, where we brought along some mannequin heads with wigs from our video to add to the set decor during our live interview. Life truly did change overnight for us, and it was such an exhilarating time for our family.

Looking back, we now see that what the Enemy meant for harm, God turned around for our good. Remember, this was the same video that was mysteriously missing from Danny's computer just days earlier. At the time, we had no idea that we were creating a massively viral video, but God did. We had no idea that the video was going to garner such a massive response and a multitude of speaking and media requests, but God did. We had no idea that giving our testimony and teaching at the conference was going to end up helping so many marriages that were on the brink of separation or divorce, but God did.

Had we been able to post the video according to *our* plan, we could've been distracted by the virality of it and potentially lost focus of the real reason we were at the conference. God made it abundantly clear that our videos are never meant to be the end goal of our ministry. The hearts of people are the end goal. The videos are simply a means to an end—the bait that we throw out to be fishers of people. They're never something we should idolize or hold in high esteem but, rather, something we should steward well in order to point others to Jesus.

We didn't know the individual stories of all the marriages represented in the room that Saturday, but God did. No matter what we all do in this life, the most important thing will always be the person right in front us. Remember, God always has someone in mind on the other side of our obedience.

The church in OKC was kind enough to send us written testimonies from people who had attended the marriage conference.

We were overwhelmed to read them all. One of these testimonies we were fortunate enough to hear in person ten months later at a church in Alvarado, Texas.

We were ministering on a Sunday morning, and after the service we were approached by a couple who had driven over three hours to come and see us. It was a couple who lived in OKC and had attended our marriage conference back in February. The husband pulled Danny aside to tell him that on the morning of our marriage conference, he and his wife had sat in their car in the church parking lot, making their plans to separate. He said that something we shared at the conference spoke directly to his heart and that without our obedience and divine intervention, his children wouldn't have a daddy at home right now.

This is the ripple effect of obedience, and this is why we will forever do our best to never again drag our feet when the Lord says, "Go."

> **Danny:** I know that our own story shouldn't surprise me, but now that we've written it out, I'm in awe of God all over again.
>
> **Kristin:** It was like He put us through an intense, real-life crash course on faith and obedience over the span of less than a year, and managed to abundantly bless us and others in the process.
>
> **Danny:** Totally. His plan is always bigger and better than what we can ever ask, think, or hope for. It can be scary and uncertain at times, but if God promises us something, then we can wholeheartedly trust that

everything will work out for our good and His glory, in His perfect timing. And when we understand that our purpose is connected to helping others, it makes the commitment to the call much greater.

Kristin: True dat.

Danny: Word.

CHAPTER 10

ARGUABLY, OUR WORST FIGHT EVER

Kristin

A few years ago, we were fortunate enough to speak at the same event as Emerson Eggerichs, bestselling author of the book *Love and Respect*. His daughter, Joy, who happens to be an old friend of mine, is the talented speaking and literary agent who managed to book the event for us. We had already read Emerson's book and held him in high esteem, so going into the event, we were like a couple of giddy little schoolgirls. We couldn't wait to meet him.

At the same time, we also hoped he wasn't a complete jerk. Has that ever happened to you? You have a hero of sorts, and then you get the opportunity to meet them in person, only to find out that they absolutely stink as a human?

Well, thankfully, Emerson's wife, Sarah, was with him on this trip. She oozes the love of Christ, and her sweet smile and warm spirit made us feel right at home.

Oh, and Emerson turned out not to be half bad either.

I kid; I joke! We fell in love with them *both*. And we assume the feeling was mutual, because after the event they told us that if we were ever in their neck of the woods up in Michigan, we were invited to bring the kids and stay for a visit.

As the Lord would have it, our annual family ski trip to Caberfae Peaks in Cadillac, Michigan, isn't far from the Eggerichses' home. So we made plans to visit them on the back end of our upcoming trip.

Danny

As we loaded things into our car at the ski lodge to head out for the ninety-minute drive to the Eggerichses' home, Kristin and I got into the beginning of what would go down as one of our worst fights in the history of our marriage. It started off seemingly small, as most fights do. Kristin was visibly irritated and frustrated with me as I packed things up, and I couldn't figure out what on earth I did that would warrant her being so mad. I tried to brush it off, but within minutes of our getting on the road, I just had to bring it up. It's difficult for me to carry on as if things are normal when they clearly are not okay.

Kristin

I don't even remember what Danny did to annoy me that day, but I do know that at that particular point in our marriage, I had developed a nasty habit of allowing myself to be highly irritated at the smallest things. This was an unhealthy pattern that started back before we even knew each other. Unhealthy patterns, when left unchecked over a long period of time—in my case, decades—can turn into spiritual strongholds. We'll talk more in the next chapter about taking thoughts captive. But I've learned that when you don't do that, you can develop fortified places in your heart, mind, and emotions that can be overthrown only by spiritual force (praying Jesus's power and authority over them).

At the time, I was unaware that this stronghold had been wreaking so much havoc in my life, but I now know being easily irritated was 100 percent what affected my severe mood swings and irritable demeanor for as long as I can remember. This attitude affected and ruined many of my past relationships and friendships, but I was spiritually blind to it for most of my life. Since I can remember, I listen to *every* negative thought that pops into my head, then make things worse by following those thoughts to perilous places that leave me assuming the worst in people and in situations, effectively leaving me in a perpetual state of worry and anxiety. Because of this emotional state, my reality was entirely different from the one Danny experienced.

The best analogy I can think of that describes having a spiritual stronghold is having a cataract. Danny just had one removed, so that's probably why I'm thinking of it, but nonetheless, the analogy works. He'd been dealing with eye issues for the past year and finally got to the bottom of what was causing him to see a constant blurred smudge out of his left eye. On his first visit to the eye specialist, he saw a computer-generated image of what the cataract looked like and how big it was. This crazy thing looked like some type of gigantic storm you would see rolling across the screen on the Weather Channel, and it almost completely covered the vision in Danny's left eye. After seeing it, I couldn't believe he had been looking at the world through that lens for so long. I mean, no wonder his driving was so bad!

But seriously, the cataract was dark, cloudy, massive, and incredibly debilitating to Danny's eyesight. Also, it was persistent. It wasn't going anywhere. The only way to remove it was through surgery.

That's what a spiritual stronghold is like. It's dark, cloudy, massive, and incredibly damaging to our soul. It's persistent. It doesn't go anywhere. The only way to remove it is through spiritual surgery, where we allow the Holy Spirit to come in and do some serious work. It requires us to fully trust in the power of God and His Word and to speak the name of Jesus over the dark things that try to weigh us down.

Back to the infamous car ride. Now, as I mentioned, I wasn't fully aware of my spiritual stronghold then, so when Danny tried to bring up that I had hurt his feelings, my reaction was the same as usual: defensive, rude, lacking empathy, and dismissive of his feelings. Then we started snapping at each other and raising our voices. By this point I couldn't even remember what initially irritated me in the first place. Now I was more upset that he chose to bring all of this up in front of the kids, knowing that most of our conflicts typically end in a nasty fight.

Danny

Yes, I lost my cool that day, just as I had done many times before. I allowed the unresolved emotional pain and hurt that I had experienced over our years together to come out in angry, harsh words toward K. Rather than praying for her and the things that were affecting her, as well as praying for my own heart to be healed and free of offense and unforgiveness, I instead permitted the pain to build, effectively allowing every wound and hurt to rule my heart. Out of the heart, my mouth spoke. I knew it was important to keep our hearts free of offense, resentment, unforgiveness, and the like, because those things often manifest in the worst of ways. But this day, I had had it.

Sadly, on that day, I just couldn't let the hurt go to find my way back. The fight got so bad that our daughter, Harper, who was eight years old at the time, yelled from the back seat, "Stop it!" Our NYC fight—the one where we took separate flights home—was bad, but this is what made this one the worst fight ever: the fact that it happened in front of our children.

It was devastating. I didn't know what to do, but given the emotional state I was in, I knew it was probably best not to continue driving. So I took the next exit and pulled into the first place I saw. There weren't many options, as we were on a stretch of highway that felt like it was in the middle of nowhere. We parked in front of a run-down Subway/gas station/arcade place. I went inside and left K and the kids in the car, hoping they would still be there when I returned. When I went inside, this place had live music that included two older gentleman playing a melancholic song on the guitar and banjo. I didn't even think it was possible to play a sad song on a banjo, but nonetheless, it only added to the misery of the moment. Plus, the fact that K wasn't there with me to get a good chuckle out of this unique scenario made things even worse.

The first thing I did was call my mentor, Trey. Trey and his wife, Ariel, have counseled Kristin and me over the years, both together and individually. I quickly explained the situation to him and told him that I wasn't sure if we should stick with our original plan of going to the Eggerichses' home, or if we should just abort the mission, go home, and attempt to work things out another time. Trey encouraged me to keep our plan and go to the Eggerichses'. He said the Eggerichses had been in ministry for forty-plus years and that this fight was exactly the type of thing they were equipped to handle.

I then left a voicemail with Emerson, explaining the situation, and asked him if he was still up for having us visit, now that, unbeknownst to us all, our overnight stay with them was about to turn into a three-day intensive counseling retreat.

He texted us back:

> **Emerson:** Please come. No problem for us. It will be fine. Sarah can play with the kids, and the three of us can chat. We've been there, done that.
>
> **Me:** Awesome. On our way.
>
> **Emerson:** You're coming to the right place.
>
> **Me:** LOL, we SO know that.
>
> **Emerson:** Sarah and I will be done with our fight by the time you get here . . .

Kristin

I'm cringing as we share this story because it certainly doesn't present the image of us we'd like you to have. This is the point where I would like to remind you that at the beginning of this book, we disclosed that we are by no means marriage experts. You remember that, right?

As I sat waiting in the car, I consoled the kids, shallowly

promising them that everything would be okay, all the while seriously contemplating driving off and leaving Danny at that run-down roadside rest stop.

Thankfully, the kids were hungry and needed to use the restroom, so I was forced to go inside and break the ice with Danny. I ordered the kids some sandwiches, and as they ate, Danny and I did our best to civilly talk through things and quickly make a plan.

He told me that he spoke with Emerson and that we basically had two choices: (1) we go home and take our issues with us, or (2) we eat some humble pie and show up at the home of one of the best Christian marriage counselors in the world and see where vulnerability takes us.

I hated both choices. While I didn't want to go home and stay stuck in the same cycle, I also didn't want to go to this couple's home, a couple whom we had met only once at this point, showing up as a hot mess. Phooey! I like to look like I have it all together . . . and now they'd know I don't!

This scenario is what we call a divine setup. Had we not had the blowup at that precise moment on our trip, we never would've spent our time with the Eggerichses working through our issues. We weren't originally planning to go see them for counseling! We were supposed to have a fun visit and spend some time getting to know them better.

But God had other plans.

Now we were forced to come clean and lay it all out on the table. The Enemy hates when darkness is brought into the light. He hates when sin is exposed, and he does everything in his power to keep us in a place of bondage, a place where we feel trapped, with seemingly no way out, enslaved to his lies.

Our marriage mentors, Sarah and Emerson Eggerichs, with our family at our house in Indiana, 2020.

Had we cancelled our visit and allowed our pride to have its way, the Enemy would've won. We weren't able to fix every problem that weekend, but we definitely gave the kingdom of darkness a black eye.

> **Danny:** Like you said, that visit didn't fix
> everything, but I remember leaving their
> home feeling relieved, equipped, and grateful

for God's providing such incredible counsel
at the exact time we needed it.

Kristin: Amen. God is into the details. For me,
it was more confirmation as to just how
important godly mentorship is, not only
before marriage but all throughout.

Danny: So you've been following through with
your weekly accountability calls?

Kristin: Wait, I thought that was your homework.

Danny: No, it was yours.

Kristin: Are you sure about that?

Danny: I know what I heard.

Kristin: I know what you *thought* you heard.

Danny: One hundred percent, I'm right.

Kristin: One hundred percent, I'm right.

Danny: All right, who's making the call to Dr. E,
me or you?

CHAPTER 11

THE BIG PICTURE

Kristin

Even though, for the better part of our marriage, Danny and I have been pursuing Jesus with all our hearts, our marriage has still been tough in many ways. While I wish they would, problems don't magically disappear once you put your faith in Christ. We've continued to have our ups and downs and crazy fights . . . er, I mean, "heated fellowships," all while trying our best to raise two humans without messing them up too much.

I point out our imperfections not to discourage but to *encourage* you. You are not alone in your current struggles. Whether your struggle is parenting, marriage, career, identity, self-esteem, finances, anxiety, depression, loss, or regret, at the end of the day, we are all in the same boat. We all desperately need Jesus every minute of every day. He is our daily bread and our very present help in times of trouble. And He, above anyone else, understands what you are going through. Jesus Himself warned us that we would have troubles in this world. In John 16:33 (NIV), He put it this way: "I have told you these things, so that in me you may have peace. In this world you will have trouble. But take heart! I have overcome the world."

There you go. Out of the mouth of God Himself. We *will* have troubles and sorrows in this life. But here's the kicker: in the same breath, Jesus promises us *peace* in the midst of it all. He offers us Himself, for He is the Prince of Peace. He promises to carry our burdens if we cast our cares on Him.

This promise also means we can stop striving for and expecting perfection in our relationships. Relationships are often complicated and messy because they are made up of people. And all people, even those who are in Christ, are imperfect. Our previous pastor used to say, "Where there's people, there's poop." To this day, I don't know if I've ever heard anything more spiritual and true than that.

We'd like to offer a bit of what we've learned about getting along and seeking God together—and not just getting along but actually *enjoying* each other. We are still learning how to be better people so we can be better spouses to each other and doing our best to lean into God every day for wisdom, strength, and humility along the way.

On my personal road to love and laughter, be it as a wife, mother, friend, sister, entrepreneur, speaker, or the countless other "titles" I've had in this life, a few things have helped me continue to grow through the good, the bad, and the ugly seasons. I've come to realize that many of these practices are what we need to continue growing in marriage as well.

1. **Daily personal recognition of my need of a Savior.**
When my pride wants to get loud, recognizing my need

of a Savior keeps me humble. It reminds me that I'm not the one in charge. I may run a business, but I'm not my own boss. I may be a mom, but I don't always have the answers. I may have a few talents, but I did nothing to deserve or earn any of them. Anything good in me is there solely because of the grace of God.

2. **Regular confession of my sin.** Confessing my sin puts the focus and onus on me, rather than blaming others for my problems. It also forces me to recognize Christ's sacrifice for and payment of my sins so that I don't fall into guilt and condemnation.

3. **Receiving God's forgiveness, love, and grace in order to have a fresh start every day.** The Enemy wants us to wake up feeling like we've already lost, but the truth is that God's mercies are new each morning. Every day that you wake up with breath in your lungs is an invitation to be a part of the greater story God is writing in your own life and in the lives of others.

4. **Keeping an attitude of gratitude.** Gratitude doesn't come naturally to me. My default setting is to look for the worst, expect the worst, and prepare for the worst. At times, I have to force myself to find things to be thankful for, both big and small, even when I don't feel like it. But feelings aren't facts! It's been said that gratitude makes what we have enough. Let that sink down into your bones for a second. I've found that when I am grateful, I see God more. I see clearly. I'm not blinded by the false promise that things of this world have to offer. I'm more aware of His presence and His goodness, and I'm filled with fresh, new hope.

5. **Be intentional about having fun.** This wasn't always top of the list for me, but it's now one of the tenets of my faith. In my opinion, humor is an essential but often neglected principle of spirituality. It's directly related to joy, which is a fruit of the spirit. Proverbs 17:22 (AMP) says, "A happy heart is good medicine and a joyful mind causes healing, but a broken spirit dries up the bones." Laughter literally causes the reciprocal effects of stress, raising good hormones and endorphin levels, while at the same time reducing stress-related hormones. When is the last time you belly-laughed? Do you have catalysts for laughter in your life and around your home? One simple way we make room for laughter as a family is by keeping a game box near the hutch by our kitchen table. After dinner, we pick something out of the box to play. It could be charades, cards, or anything that gets the fun flowing. Let's not be so deadly serious about our faith that we forget to be joyfully alive in it!

6. **Remember God's faithfulness and dream together.** Don't let your present struggles become so magnified that you either forget all the good God has already done or allow it to diminish your hope for the future. Take regular trips down memory lane by watching old videos or flipping through photo albums and recall beautiful memories you've made together. Go on dream dates where you talk vision and possibilities for the future. Keep hope alive!

Now, by no means have I mastered all these areas. It's a daily fight for victory, and I definitely didn't know all of this when Danny and I were first married. We both still have a lot more to battle and a lot more to learn, but nonetheless, we're here as two people who, although we may continually fall short, are held together by a loving, faithful, and powerful God. Our heart is to encourage you and inspire you to fight for your spouse and your family and to live out a marriage full of passion, conviction, and unwavering commitment. We're not ordained preachers or teachers with seminary degrees and such. We're just two flawed people who, by the grace of God, have been saved, redeemed, and set free. We are together today *only* because of Jesus and His relentless pursuit of our hearts.

We've been to tons of marriage seminars, workshops, conferences, and counseling sessions, not because we are studious, spiritual, or diligent in doing research for this ministry "call" that God has placed on our lives but because we've desperately needed help. Throughout our counseling sessions, marriage seminars, research, and personal experience, we've learned that how you view marriage, and your beliefs regarding marriage, will ultimately determine your success in marriage. We like to say, "You gotta

One of our "Date Night with Kristin and Danny" events at Emmanuel Church in Greenwood, Indiana, 2019.

know your *why* or you're gonna lose your *way*," which is true for most things in life, but it especially holds true in marriage. The Bible says, "Where there is no vision, the people perish" (Proverbs 29:18 KJV). This lack of vision that the Bible talks about may in fact be why a lot of marriages are failing these days. Perhaps if more people were tethered to God's greater vision and purpose for marriage, we would see more couples staying in the fight.

We not only need vision for our marriage, but we also need to understand why God created marriage in the first place. There are obvious reasons—procreating a godly legacy and the blessing of experiencing lifelong companionship—but I'm going to suggest two lesser-known purposes that have had a profound impact on us.

Marriage Was Designed to Make Us Holy

The subtitle of Gary Thomas's book *Sacred Marriage* asks, "What if God designed marriage to make us holy more than to make us happy?" It's a profound proposition, and one with which we happen to wholeheartedly agree. If this blessed union was God's idea in the first place, then marriage *must* have a much higher purpose than our own individual happiness or our own personal satisfaction. God's ways and thoughts are higher than ours, and keeping His perspective on marriage is crucial if we want our marriages to be fulfilled and long-lasting.

But this higher plan and greater purpose can't be attained without going through a *process* . . . and an often painful one at that. The Bible describes this process as two becoming one (Genesis 2:24). It's what the apostle Paul calls "a great mystery" (Ephesians 5:32), and it doesn't happen overnight. Joining two lives together is a lifelong endeavor, and we can't do it successfully without God's help.

Part of two becoming one involves dying to yourself. The specific phrase "dying to yourself" isn't in the Bible, but the idea is woven throughout. Essentially, it's disciplining yourself and your flesh (your carnal nature) not to fight for its own way. That's probably the most painful part of the entire two-becoming-one process. But let me let you in on a little secret that makes the pain endurable: it's pain *with a purpose*. Or better yet, pain *with a divine purpose*.

Here are some of the ways God encourages us to "die to ourselves," or to kill our own selfish desires:

- "He must increase, but I must decrease" (John 3:30).
- "I have been crucified with Christ; it is no longer I who live, but Christ lives in me; and the life which I now live in the flesh I live by faith in the Son of God, who loved me and gave Himself for me" (Galatians 2:20).
- "I affirm, by the boasting in you which I have in Christ Jesus our Lord, I die daily" (1 Corinthians 15:31).

Dying to yourself is getting to a place where you sincerely desire more of God's way and less of your own. I love the way Paul Tripp communicates this idea in his book *What Did You Expect?*: Marriage was designed to "drive each of us away from habits of self-reliance into patterns of dependency on God."[1] Now, I don't know about you, but that quote cuts me to the core. Because I've prided myself on independence and self-sufficiency, moving away from self-reliance messes with my whole life plan.

The truth is, even as Christians, we will always battle the

---

1. Paul David Tripp, *What Did You Expect? Redeeming the Realities of Marriage* (Wheaton, IL: Crossway, 2010), 67–68.

tyranny of self. We must constantly push our flesh down and earnestly cry out, "Not *my* will, but *yours* be done, Lord!" That's the heart posture it takes to have a marriage that endures. Otherwise, we end up making marriage all about *ourselves* and *our* wants rather than about God and what He wants.

Nothing has made me realize my desperate need for God more than my marriage. It's one area where I can't "act as if." And when you know that God is birthing something through you and your spouse that you could never achieve on your own, you are motivated to stay in the fight. Every time you resist the urge to run away or throw in the towel, you develop what I like to call marital grit, the ability to persevere through hard times. *Grit* isn't a word you hear a lot these days, because frankly, our culture is losing grit at an alarming pace. Instead of putting in the work when things get tough, many simply quit when any amount of effort is required. But grit says, "I ain't quitting no matter what." Gritty people are the ones who achieve long-term goals. They don't buy into the next-best-thing mentality, and they aren't afraid of putting in extra hours. They show up early and stay late. They don't quit until the job is done. They focus on the deep, inner work in themselves because they know that's what builds strength and stamina.

Here is a simple prayer to ask the Lord to grace you with the grit you need to endure anything life throws your way. Now, I must warn you that this is a super-deep, hyperspiritual, insanely intense prayer, so read it with caution:

Lord . . .
    make me gritty . . .
so I don't quitty.

There it is. You were warned.

Marriage Was Designed to Put the Gospel on Display

I believe that one of the reasons God created marriage was not only to help us know Him better but also to help others know Him better. The good news is that even when we were dead in our sins, Christ still loved us, chose to die for us, and made a way for us to spend eternity with God. When we accept Jesus as our Lord and Savior, our sins are laid upon Him, and His righteousness (which we all need but don't deserve) is laid upon us. Marriage is meant to be a reflection of this "great exchange." It's meant to be one of the greatest tools to point others to Christ. When we look for ways to bless and serve each other, forgive each other, and sacrificially love each other, we put the redemptive story of the gospel on display for the world to see. Husbands, when you love your wives as Christ loves the church (even when they don't deserve it), you put the gospel on display. Wives, when you respect and honor your husbands as unto the Lord (even when they don't deserve it), you put the gospel on display. Nothing speaks louder to the world about the goodness of God than a marriage submitted to God and to each other.

I realize this is all easier said than done, especially if you've allowed offense, selfishness, and immaturity to suck the love out of your relationship. But often in marriage, it's not that we don't love each other enough; it's that we don't love God and allow Him to love us like we should. In other words, when we don't love and adore Christ the way we are created to worship Him, then we aren't capable of loving and honoring each other as we should. It's that simple. So it only makes sense that more we fall in love with Jesus, and the more we receive His love for us, the more able we are to love those around us well.

It's crucial that we regularly examine our own heart instead of trying to change our spouse's heart. "Create in *me* a clean heart, O God, and renew a steadfast spirit within *me*" (Psalm 51:10, emphasis added). Growth and progress come only when we stop pointing fingers and start confessing our own shortcomings and weaknesses.

Here are a few questions to regularly ask yourself:

- Do you celebrate your spouse as one who was created in God's image, or are you too busy trying to recreate them in your own image?
- Have you allowed the good things you once admired about your spouse to become things you now despise? Have you started keeping a record of all the wrong things they do?
- What is your heart motivation when you show love toward your spouse? Are you secretly expecting something in return?

If you need to gain a higher vision for your marriage, remembering these things may be helpful:

- **Your spouse is a fellow image-bearer of God.** Because of this, your spouse is *always* worthy of dignity, honor, and respect.
- At the same time, your spouse is **a fellow sinner, who, *like you*, needs Jesus**. (Once we confess Jesus as Lord and are saved by grace through faith, we are no longer slaves to sin. But as we are reminded in 1 John 1:8 (NIV), "If we claim to

be without sin, we deceive ourselves and the truth is not in us." For that reason, I consider myself and fellow believers in Christ *sinners* who are saved from their sin.)

When we get these two views right, positive marital change is not only possible, it's inevitable. When we get these two views wrong, our marriage worsens. If we don't see our spouse as a fellow image-bearer of God, we stop handling their heart with care. We stop giving grace. If we don't see our spouse as a fellow sinner, we withhold forgiveness and heap on judgment. We become deceived by our own self-righteousness. We stop thinking that we are the one who needs changing and at the same time become frustrated that our spouse doesn't see their need for change.

It's important to have regular theological check-ins like this with ourselves because the ways of the world and culture can creep in without our knowing it. You've probably heard sentiments like, "Marriage is about give and take," or, "It's a 50/50 partnership." That may seem like sound advice on the surface, but who wants halfsies when it comes to love? That philosophy may be well-meaning, but it's not rooted in the kind of love that's meant to endure, outlast, and overcome. It won't transform, purify, renew, or sustain us.

The love that causes a marriage to thrive and not just survive isn't 50/50. It's 100/0. It empties itself, while remaining full. It dies to itself and puts the needs of others first. It never insists on its own way. It believes the best and keeps no record of wrongs. It's never offended nor offensive. It's patient, kind, comforting, and eternal, and it's so powerful that it obliterates fear. It suffers long and never fails. It's full of grit and endurance.

> In the beginning was the Word, and the Word was with God,
> and the Word was God.
>
> —JOHN 1:1

> God is love.
>
> —1 JOHN 4:8

From these verses, we know that:

- The Word is God.
- God is love.
- The Word is love.

Therefore, God and His Word, who are both love, are the *only* ones qualified to teach us about love. Hollywood isn't qualified. Pornography isn't qualified. Culture isn't qualified. Christ, and Christ alone, who was the Word made flesh, is the only one qualified to set the example for us. His love went the distance for us. His love doesn't take; it only gives. His love doesn't hold us down; it lifts us up. His love endures forever and ever.

This higher love that causes a marriage to survive *and* thrive is God Himself, for He *is* love. If we allow love to fully govern our hearts, minds, marriages, and relationships as it was intended to from the beginning of time, we would see some crazy-awesome, mind-blowing, supernatural transformation in every relationship in our lives. This kind of love can't be manufactured or birthed out of our own strength. It comes when we abide in the Vine and let God fill us up daily so that we can continually pour out love on those around us.

Kristin: After reading my own words, I feel like I just need to say that I love you you, babe.

Danny: Aw, thanks.

Kristin: No, really. Even though you totally don't deserve it, I love you anyway.

Danny: Thanks . . . I think?

Kristin: What I meant to say is that I want to own and acknowledge my part in our problems. I mean, I brought just as much sin and funk and junk into our relationship as you did. So I want to walk in humility, focus on my own sin and desperate need for Jesus, and say that the biggest problem in our marriage isn't you. It will always be me.

Danny: Wow. That's incredible to hear you say that.

Kristin: And this is where you say that the biggest problem in our marriage will always be . . .

Danny: You.

Kristin: Danny!

Danny: Oh, sorry. Wait, *me*. I for sure meant to say me.

CHAPTER 12

HELP, WE'RE DIFFERENT!

Kristin: It often surprises people when we tell them that you and I are different in so many ways.

Danny: Totally, because based on our videos, it's easy to assume that we're just two peas in a pod, laughing and cracking jokes all the time.

Kristin: But anyone can look like they have it all together in a three-minute edited video clip.

Danny: Exactly. The truth is that there are twenty-three hours and fifty-seven minutes left in the day where you and I approach life and situations very differently.

Kristin: We're still alike in a lot of areas, like our shared faith, our senses of humor, our love of coffee and episodes of *The Office* . . .

Danny: Our love of travel, documentaries, and long walks on the beach . . .

Kristin: Hold up . . . when have you ever taken me for a long walk on the beach?

Danny: In my head. And it was amazing.

Kristin: Despite these similarities, a lot of times, like right now, it still feels like we're on totally different pages.

Danny: Maybe even different planets.

Kristin: So, for instance, I'm a suburban girl—

Danny: and I'm an inner-city kid.

Kristin: I'm impulsive—

Danny: and I . . .

Kristin: take your sweet time with things?

Danny: Yes, I'm definitely the more patient of the two of us. You're ready to move on an idea or project at the first mention of it.

Kristin: Yeah, and you're over there sitting and meditating on it, day and night, night and day.

Danny: That's what I call wisdom.

Kristin: That's what I call annoying. Let's just keep going with the list. I'm a binge-watcher.

Danny: I'm a one-or-two-episodes-at-a-time kinda guy.

Kristin: I love hot and spicy. Give me all the jalapeños.

Danny: I like to keep things mild to medium. Hold the jalapeños.

Kristin: I grew up on rock and roll.

Danny: I grew up on R&B.

Kristin: I like to sleep in.

Danny: I'm an early riser.

Kristin: I'm really smart—
Danny: and I'm . . . wait a second . . .

Kristin

Years ago, we each took a personality test—the kind that asks you pages and pages of questions and then, at the end of the test, puts you into a category. That category comes complete with a list of all your strengths, which is wonderful to read through, and a list of all your weaknesses, which is not wonderful to read through. Some of these personality tests are a little too accurate for my liking. I'm not sure, but I think whoever is making these tests may be dabbling a wee bit into witchcraft. I'm not saying they're all in, but they definitely have one leg on the broomstick.

Danny

Back when we took these tests, I was on staff at our home church in Los Angeles. Our church, like many organizations, administered these tests to build teams more effectively. So when I was asked to take one as part of a leadership retreat, K asked me to bring a copy home so she could take one too. Our results were a little unsettling, yet not completely surprising. They confirmed that we're not only different but completely *opposite* in almost every way possible. In fact, the results blatantly conveyed that if people with my personality type want peace in their lives, we should stay away from K's personality type. Thanks for the tip, but we were already four years into our marriage at this point, so staying away from each other wasn't exactly a viable option.

Kristin

That's the thing about these tests. Most, if not all, of them leave God out of the equation. With Him, all things are possible, including my personality type and Danny's personality type living in peace with each other. God made no mistake with the personality He gave you. And He's not at all surprised by whom you married either. He's not looking down from heaven going, "Wait a second! Kristin and Danny? Oh no! How on earth as it is in heaven did those two personality types end up together?" No, no, no. When you've sought God's way (to love sacrificially), you can be sure that you and your spouse were put together by divine design. And guess what, those differences you guys have? They were put there by our Creator *on* purpose, *for* a purpose.

> **Danny:** The major difference between us that the test nailed on the head was in reference to our motivators. I'm a people person, through and through. Relationships are the biggest motivator in my life.
>
> **Kristin:** And I'm a task-oriented person. Results are the biggest motivator in my life.
>
> **Danny:** Now, valuing relationships over everything else doesn't mean I don't have goals. It's just that if I meet someone on the way to achieving a goal, I may forget about the goal. I get goal amnesia. Then I come home and my wife asks if all my errands were completed, and I'm like, "Well, no, but guess what? I made a new friend!"

Kristin: Exactly. And being results-driven doesn't mean I don't like people. It's that I don't have time for small talk or chit-chat on the way to achieving the goal. I'm sort of a goal Nazi. And anyone who crosses my path on the way to achieving my goal is left with a footprint on their neck.

Kristin

Here's an extremely exaggerated real-life scenario from several years back about how these differences play out in our marriage.

I'm at home one night, making banana pancakes for dinner, because breakfast for dinner is *always* a good idea. But when I start cooking, I realize I'm out of bananas. Danny jumps up and shouts, "No problem, babe! I'll head to the grocery store to pick some up." After all these years, I finally figured out why Danny loves to do the grocery shopping: because there are *people* at the grocery store.

I quickly do the calculations in my head . . . that's ten minutes to the grocery store, two mins to run in and buy them, and ten minutes back home. "Okay, D, so I'll see you in twenty-two minutes!"

He happily heads out. I continue with dinner. Thirty minutes go by and Danny's not back yet. I think, "Okay, he got stopped at the train tracks. No prob. I can hold things for five more minutes."

Another twenty minutes go by and he's still not back. These days, I'd text him, and if he's not trapped under something heavy, he'll respond and apologize. But an hour goes by and he's still not back. At this point I'm not at all concerned with what happened or wondering where Danny is. I know *exactly* where he is. Somewhere between walking into the grocery store and walking back out to his car, he met someone. Let's call him Bob. He and Bob start talking. Danny asks him a million questions, not because he is trying to make my life difficult but because he is genuinely interested in Bob's life. He finds out Bob needs prayer. He prays for him. He finds out Bob doesn't know God. He asks if he wants to know God by accepting Jesus into his heart. Bob says yes. They pray again. He invites Bob to church. They exchange information, and before you know it, both he and Bob are on the way back to enjoy some banana pancakes.

But guess what? There are no banana pancakes *because I didn't have any bananas.* At this moment, all I want in life is banana pancakes, but since Danny was too busy being the hands and feet of Jesus, I am forced to settle for plain ol' regular, banana-free pancakes.

Yes, I realize how shallow I seem in this scenario, but when our selfishness is confronted, crazy things can manifest. Please tell me I'm not the only one.

You can't always have things when you want them, the way you want them, and also expect to have a successful marriage. I've learned that I can still make my lists and do my best to check things off, but I've also learned to hold my lists with an open palm. I may make my plans, but it's the Lord who orders my steps. Those moments when a Bob presents himself and our convenience is inconvenienced, we have a choice to make. Is our choice going to further God's kingdom or our own little kingdom?

In the end, being results driven can mean we are irritated by things that don't matter much at all. But somehow, someway, we manage to allow the silliest things to get underneath our skin. As I mentioned earlier, when Danny and I first started living together, one of the things that bothered me most was the way he loaded the dishwasher. Every time I would open it and see the chaos of glasses and dishes strewn about with no order at all, I would think, "What kind of idiot would load the dishwasher this way? Oh my! I live with that idiot! If he can't even load the dishwasher correctly, what else can he not do right?" And then I would start looking for all the ways in which Danny did things different from me. In my mind, different equaled wrong. And guess what? We will *always* find what we are looking for. Anything put under a magnifying glass will appear bigger than it actually is. And that's what it's like when we intentionally look for flaws in people. The littlest things will irritate us more than they should because we are hyperfocused on them. And then we are so caught up in the weeds that we can no longer see the forest for the trees.

Kristin as Daniel LaRusso and Danny as Johnny Lawrence while filming our "80s Movies" lip sync video, 2019.

This is what Danny and I refer to as low-level warfare. This is where the Enemy wants to keep us—fighting insignificant battles. God wants us operating at a much higher level. I love the way the apostle Paul put it in the book of Colossians. He said, "If you're serious about living this new resurrection life with Christ, *act* like it. Pursue the things over which Christ presides. Don't shuffle along, eyes to the ground, absorbed with the things right in front of you. Look up, and be alert to what is going on around Christ—that's where the action is. See things from *his* perspective" (Colossians 3:1–2 MSG).

When we live in this place, up high where there is rarefied air, these low-level insignificant scuffles have no room to breathe. They are choked out by a higher calling.

All we have to do is shift our perspective and look up. So instead of being irritated with the *way* Danny loaded the dishwasher, how about I praise God for the simple fact that Danny loaded it in the first place? Boom. Not today, Satan.

No matter how different you and your spouse are, we want to encourage you to start embracing your differences as gifts from our Creator. They were put there on purpose to make you both better—to sharpen you, form you, mold you, and shape you ultimately to look more like Christ. Your spouse is your iron-sharpens-iron gift from God. Your marriage can be one of the greatest tools of spiritual refinement in your life, *if* you choose to see it that way.

PRACTICAL WAYS TO CELEBRATE THE DIFFERENCES

If we don't intentionally celebrate our spouse, chances are we will merely tolerate them. Can you imagine if on your wedding day your spouse promised to simply tolerate you for the rest of your life?

Danny: I, Danny, take thee, Kristin, to tolerate all the things that annoy me for the rest of my life.

Kristin: I, Kristin, take thee, Danny, forsaking all others, to tolerate your frustrating habits and ignorant opinions for the rest of my life.

Danny: I vow to tolerate you in sickness and in health, even during your mood swings and attempts to control every fiber of my being.

Kristin: I vow to tolerate you until your untimely death does us part.

Would somebody please stand up and object already? Those vows may sound ridiculous, but sadly, many marriages get stuck at Toleration Station. If couples aren't careful, the next stop is Low-Grade Irritation Station, where pretty much everything their spouse does bothers them to some degree.

If you're in this place, or want to avoid getting there, here are some ways we have found to safeguard against it.

1. Celebrate Your Spouse with Your Thoughts

Our thoughts are where most things in our lives, good or bad, begin. What do you regularly think about when it comes to your spouse? The Bible tells us in 2 Corinthians 10:5 (NIV) to "take captive every thought to make it obedient to Christ." For some people, that can feel like a full-time job, depending on how out of control their thought life is. The Bible also tells us, "As he thinks in his heart, so is he" (Proverbs 23:7). Essentially that means what you magnify in your mind eventually grows in your life. That's how powerful our thoughts are.

Changing your thought life is difficult, especially if unhealthy patterns have developed over a long period of time, but it's not impossible. One of God's promises to us is that we can *renew* our minds. We can kill old ways of thinking. Despite what the world tells us, people can change. If you are willing to saturate your mind with God's Word and yield your spirit to His Holy Spirit, change isn't just possible, it's inevitable.

2. Celebrate Your Spouse with Your Words

Celebrating your spouse with your words is the second point because after you've done the necessary work on your thought life, your words should follow suit. Remember, what we think, we eventually become, which means our thinking affects our heart, our innermost being. And the Bible tells us that "out of the abundance of the heart the mouth speaks" (Matthew 12:34). So if there is anything icky in your heart, do what King David did and cry out to God, "Create in me a clean heart, O God, and renew a right spirit within me" (Psalm 51:10 ESV). Once our words are out in the atmosphere, the damage can be catastrophic. Are the words you speak to your spouse meant to build them up or tear them down? Are they encouraging or discouraging?

Encouraging words go a long way to build trust and strengthen relationships. They are like spiritual oxygen, helping others function at a higher level. They do a body, and a marriage, good. Also, it's not always what we say but how we say it. Your tone matters. Even if you need to work through conflict or a misunderstanding, you can still choose to speak the truth with love. Get away to calm down, or even just take a moment to settle and pray.

3. Celebrate Your Spouse with Your Actions

Words matter, but they're in vain if our actions don't back them up. The apostle James said, "Faith without works is dead" (James 2:20), meaning there should be some type of action to confirm that we really believe what we say we believe. Jesus Himself said, "If you love me, you will obey" (John 14:15 GW). Obedience is the action that proves what we say is in our hearts. Do your actions support the notion that you celebrate your spouse? Do you have eyes only for them? Do you honor them with how you spend your time? Do you find ways to serve them? Do you support any of their interests or hobbies by joining in or asking questions? Do you send them a text or leave a sweet note simply to let them know you are thinking of them?

If you and your spouse are different, start celebrating! God wouldn't have brought you two together if you weren't *better* together. Those differences aren't in the way of His plan; they are part of His plan to grow and better you. He is using them to bring forth refinement, blessing, and spiritual growth in your life. In the end you will look more like Christ because of the glorious gift of your wonderful, amazing, magnificent, fantastic, superbly *different* spouse.

CHAPTER 13

MARRIAGE IS A TEAM SPORT

Kristin

During our moments of "heated fellowship"—when I'm on my soapbox of trying to be right and win the argument at all costs with my verbal ninja skills—Danny will now come over to me, put his hand on my shoulder, and say, "K, remember, we're on the same team." He'll look around the house and remind me that it's just the two of us there. No one else is around. There's no grand jury that's going to decide who wins this argument in the end. It's a simple yet profound reminder for all the married couples out there: remember, you're on the same team.

Kristin as Maverick and Danny as Goose while prepping to film a Top Gun parody for our "80s Movies" lip sync video, 2019.

Danny

I discovered at an early age that when I played any team sport, I was plugging into something bigger than myself. I quickly learned that winning the game or any success we had on the field wasn't all about me. One of the key ways to win as a team is to put everyone in position to do what they do best. On the contrary, one of the key ways to fail as a team is to have a bunch of individuals focused on just doing their own thing.

Likewise, the best way to fail at our relationships is to make them all about me. If I choose to make them all about me and my wants, then *I* am at the center of my relationship, which means I've lost God as my anchor. Now God isn't in His rightful place, and I ultimately don't win.

From the time I was five years old through high school, I was a three-sport athlete, playing football, basketball, and baseball, but my favorite sport was football. I always looked at football as the ultimate team sport. In my opinion, no other sport epitomizes the meaning of team more than football. In baseball, a great pitcher can individually dominate the game. In basketball, there are isolation plays where it's the best player going one-on-one with the defender. But in football, all eleven men on the team have to do their part on every individual play, or things often don't go as planned.

Every Successful Team Puts in the Work

Another life lesson I learned from playing team sports was the importance of training and preparation. Marriage is the greatest decision you will ever make outside of accepting Christ into your life, so why not prepare by getting the necessary tools to have a successful marriage? We train for everything else, right?—sports, school, jobs. Why not do that for your marriage, which was designed to reflect Christ to the world?

When preparing to play a game, my team often referred to it as "going to war." This was because we were facing an opponent who would do anything and everything to prevent us from achieving our goals and winning the game. They wanted to steal victory from us. So we would spend all week between games training, preparing, and studying. We made sure that we were physically and mentally ready to go to battle. We studied our opponent by watching film from other games they had played in order to learn their strengths, weaknesses, and tendencies. They too spent the week studying us and our tactics. Both teams used all the tools at their disposal to best position themselves for victory.

Every Successful Team Studies Their Opponent

In life and relationships, especially in marriage, we face an enemy as well. This enemy has been around since the dawn of time, which means he's had a long time to study us and our habits, and he's a master at exploiting our weaknesses. His number one goal is "to steal and kill and destroy" (John 10:10), and he isn't satisfied with just scoring a few points here and there. He wants total domination. Satan would love nothing more than to create a mockery out of what God brought together in you and your spouse. Your marriage was meant to shine by reflecting God's glory to the world, and Satan can't stand that. He wants all the glory for himself.

Marriages will always be a spiritual target of the Enemy, so it's important to know the spiritual battle you are up against when you say, "I do." From that point on, Satan wants us to focus on fighting with each other so that we are too busy, distracted, and exhausted to fight him. To counter this attack, we must learn to fight *for* each other, not *with* each other. You and your spouse are on the same team; therefore, you have a common enemy—and it's not each other. The apostle Paul warns us in Galatians 5:15: "If you bite and devour each other, watch out or you will be destroyed by each other." When we destroy each other, we do Satan's work for him.

Have you ever watched a sports game and seen a team turn on each other? There's often a lot of shouting, pointing fingers, and shifting blame. It's a telltale sign that the other team has found their weakness and now has the upper hand. Bickering within a team signifies that it is falling apart from the inside out, and now it's just a matter of the opponent keeping them in this state until the clock runs out.

In marriage, a house divided cannot stand. Jesus warned us of this Himself. We must be committed to unity and oneness before stepping onto the field, or the Enemy will undoubtedly win.

Every Successful Team Has a Great Leader

I played quarterback on my football teams for many years. The quarterback is the leader of the team and often determines how successful the team will be. The QB is responsible for calling the play in the huddle, leading the team down the field, and is vital in keeping up team morale.

Being a vocal leader was one of the greatest contributions I was able to offer the teams I played for. I loved getting to know my teammates and learning the best way to motivate each player. Because of my leadership position, I saw firsthand that the team would go in the direction of my words. For example, things wouldn't turn out so well if I stepped into the huddle offering zero confidence or encouraging words. "All right, guys. I'm probably not going to have any accuracy when throwing the ball for the rest of the game. Where's my receiver? Yeah, let's be honest, you're the worst receiver in the entire league. You couldn't catch a cold. And our opponent? They're simply better, stronger, smarter, and faster in every way. Now, let's get out there and prepare for the worst. Ready? Break!"

A receiver is one of the QB's greatest assets. In that illustration, I essentially just took one of my most valuable players out of the game. In marriage, your spouse is your most valuable teammate. The words we speak, and the tone in which we speak them, matter greatly. Our spouse's success is our success. Their failure is our failure. The words we speak have the power to determine whether we sink or swim together. Our words carry power, on and off the field. The words we speak either bless or curse any team dynamic we find ourselves in. The Bible explains it like this in Proverbs 18:21 (NIV): "The tongue has the power of life and death, and those who love it will eat its fruit." And in the book of James, the tongue is likened to the rudder of a ship. Although it may be small in size, it still has the power to single-handedly change the course of the entire ship. Our teams (including our marriage and family) will go in the direction of our word, so it's vital that we speak life.

No matter how bleak things may have seemed, it was my job as the offensive leader on the field to find a way to rally the troops. I'd say something like, "All right, guys. This is our moment. We're prepared for this. This is what we worked for all season. This is why we lift all the weights and run all the sprints. Where's my receiver? It's not too late to turn things around. You've got hands of glue, baby! We're gonna march down the field, score a touch-down, and win this game! Ready? Break!"

Every Successful Team Has a Great Coach

Motivating and inspiring each other is much easier when you know what you are working toward. When you look back at the greatest sports teams in history, most had a great coach at the helm. Great coaches make the vision clear and are effective in communicating the goals of the team. They consistently achieve winning results because they know how to motivate their players to work well with one another.

K and I have been blessed to have great "coaches" in our marriage. Even before we were married, we knew the benefit of wise counsel. We have mentors who counsel us through some of the toughest valleys and celebrate with us once we've reached the mountaintop. We openly share our struggles with them, heed their advice, do our best to make the necessary adjustments, debrief, and do it all over again. They've seen us at our best and our worst and are still *for* us. They want us to grow. They want us to succeed. They remind us of the greater purpose in the two of us being together.

While coaches hold the team accountable, having other influences in your life that focus on your individual development is important as well. One my closest mentors encouraged me early in my walk with the Lord to establish what he calls a "power climate." Some people call it an "inner circle," but for me, power climate is more apropos. A power climate is made up of close, trusted friends who are full of faith and are committed to helping protect and strengthen your spiritual walk. They see things that others, even you sometimes, can't. They do more than just hold you accountable. They strengthen you, encourage you, check you, and lift you higher. They are the atmosphere-changers in your life. They don't sit and wallow in your pity party with you. They always bring things back to Christ and His kingdom and the part you play in advancing His purposes here on earth. After I spend time with my power climate, I'm always a better me when I come back home to K.

If you're married right now, your spouse is your teammate and greatest asset. An old proverb says, "If you want to go fast, go alone. If you want to go far, go together." You and your spouse can accomplish far more together than you ever could on your own. Look for ways to position each other to shine. Focus on your spouse's strengths, not their weaknesses. Evaluate yourself, and elevate your spouse. In other words, work on bettering and changing yourself, and in turn, both of you will be lifted higher.

Now go forth and be the best teammate you can be!

> **Kristin:** That was good, babe. So what position do I play on your team?
>
> **Danny:** You're like the team manager.
>
> **Kristin:** Ooh, a manager position. That sounds important.
>
> **Danny:** Well, we're talking football here, so just make sure my jersey's washed, and bring me some water.
>
> **Kristin:** Hold up, what?
>
> **Danny:** Don't worry, you're an extremely valuable part of the team. You just don't actually get on the field.

Kristin: I'm confused. Did you want to sleep on the couch tonight?

Danny: Girl, I'm just playin'. . . . You know you're my MVP, on and off the field.

Kristin: That's what I'm talking about.

Danny: All right, huddle up. Let's get out there, have some fun, play together as a team, and march down the field to victory.

Kristin: Let's do it! Oh, and remember . . .

K & D: *Laughter is the best medicine!*

FREQUENTLY ASKED QUESTIONS

How did you become "YouTubers"?

Danny: This is by far one of our most frequently asked questions.

Kristin: Since our videos went viral on Facebook, wouldn't that technically make us more "Facebookers" than YouTubers?

Danny: Well, yes, if you want to get technical, Facebookers would be more accurate than YouTubers. But since Facebookers isn't really a thing and doesn't exactly roll off the tongue, we'll just have to stick with YouTubers.

Kristin: Okay . . . wait! What about "FaceTubers"?

Danny: Ooh, I like it. It's official then . . . we're FaceTubers!

Danny

Back in 2015 we were driving home from an event one evening, listening to the radio, when the song "I Wanna Dance with Somebody" by Whitney Houston came on. Instantly, we were both feeling the groove and belting out the lyrics because, c'mon, who doesn't love Whitney, a.k.a. "The Voice"? She is hands down my favorite female singer of all time.

So, as we were jammin' and singing at the top of our lungs in the car, Kristin suggested that we make a lip sync video to this song. Now, even though we had never talked about making lip sync videos per se, her suggestion wasn't out of the blue either. For me, this was speaking directly to my heart because at eleven years old, I took home second place at the annual lip sync contest at a local street fair in my neighborhood for performing Whitney Houston's "Saving All My Love for You." My rendition came complete with a wig, a fabulous 1980s dress, and props, including a cooking pot with a handwritten note taped on it that said "love" for the part of the song that says, "We'll be making love the whole night through," at which point I stirred the "love" pot in my attempt to add humor and make the lyric more age appropriate. So, needless to say, I was all-in at Kristin's suggestion. We had long felt the pull of combining our efforts and working together in some capacity someday, but never had a clear vision of how that dream would play out. We flirted with things like creating a variety show of sorts, to loftier dreams of starting our own family-friendly television network. But, as with any dream, you have to start somewhere, sometimes with what you have in your hands at the moment. For us, that was an iPhone.

A couple of mornings later, we woke up early around six

o'clock to start filming our very first video. Our plan was to film it before the kids woke up so we would have fewer distractions, but our son, Holt, was a year and a half old at the time and an early riser. On this day of course he decided to wake up right as we were about to push Record.

We were already dressed in our eighties outfits, and K's rockin' blue eye shadow and bright lipstick to boot, so we *had* to make this video happen. We started strategizing on how we could keep Holt occupied and came up with the genius solution of strapping our iPad around the bars of his crib with *Toy Story* cued up. We set a bowl of "puffs" in front of him and told him that Mommy and Daddy would be right outside filming a video.

We took the baby monitor with us, propped our iPhone at the base of our garage, turned on Whitney, and started lip-syncing and dancing in our driveway in the wee hours of the morning. We had a blast, and by the end of filming, both kids were sitting together watching Mommy and Daddy dancing in front of their phone while wearing crazy outfits. It definitely seemed strange to them at the time, but now it's just par for the course in our family.

Once we finished the video, it was time to edit it all together. Now, five years into making videos full-time, I'm confident as an editor. But at the time, I had never edited anything and had taken only a few free classes at our local Apple store that came with the purchase of my laptop. So I didn't exactly feel prepared or equipped to start editing, but there was no other option. If we wanted to start making our own content on a regular basis, we had to wear all the hats.

Once I completed the video, it was time to upload it to our social media platforms. At the time, we had only a few hundred people following our accounts, but to our surprise, the "I Wanna Dance with Somebody" lip sync quickly garnered forty thousand views and was reshared on popular social channels and websites, like KIIS FM radio in Los Angeles. We were blown away by the positive response, and it encouraged us to keep making more videos.

A few weeks later, we posted our second lip sync video to the 1990s hit "Gonna Make You Sweat (Everybody Dance Now)," which we filmed primarily in our kitchen. Once again, we received positive feedback and the video surpassed forty thousand views. We loved the "feel good" impact we were having, plus, making videos together as a family was amazing! We continued shooting videos, but because we both had other jobs and commitments, our posts were sporadic. Our hearts were telling us to drop everything and to start putting all our efforts into making videos, but we were still living in LA and had to continue paying the bills. We had no idea how this "social media thing" worked in terms of making an actual living doing it, so for a while, it was simply a hobby.

We were able to give energy to this new vision only when we had the time, which at that point in our lives while juggling freelance gigs and two small children was after nine o'clock at night when the kids went to bed. We would fire up the coffee and bang out as much as we could. Everything, from planning future videos to securing web domains, building our website from scratch, creating marketing materials, and curating posts all happened during those midnight hours. We were regularly going to bed around two o'clock in the morning and getting little to no sleep. Couple that with the fact that Holt was a fickle sleeper and woke up several times throughout the night, so we were exhausted, but also exhilarated by putting our hands to this new endeavor.

We continued to work around the clock for the next six months. While there is some gratification knowing that we managed to grind our way through laying the groundwork for what was to come over the next five years, the reality was that there was zero financial return on our creative efforts at that point in time. We realized that if we had any chance of making a living from providing feel-good, family-friendly content, we needed to be creating content full-time.

That's when chapter 8, "Faith Can Make You Move," came into play, where God led us to Indiana and where we became full-time FaceTubers.

How do you keep the laughter in your marriage?

Kristin: People often ask us this after one of our live events or after watching one of our videos, and it's an important question. But I'd like to point out that while we fight to keep laughter alive in our marriage and family, we don't sit around laughing all day, every day. At the same time, if laughter isn't flowing or seems absent for an extended period, that may mean something bigger needs to be addressed. Most of the time, laughing at or with someone is difficult when unresolved pain, hurt, or conflict is present. For example, Danny's the funniest person I know, but when I'm upset at him, I don't care if he just did the funniest thing on the planet. I am *not* laughing.

Danny: Yeah, you've been a tough crowd a time or two.

Kristin: Welp, you've been a jerk a time or two.

Danny: Touché.

Kristin: For us, we keep the laughter in our marriage by keeping our hearts light and free of what we like to call "laugh blockers." These develop from wounds and offenses that build up over time (hurts, resentments, bitterness, unforgiveness), and they eventually make it difficult to laugh or have any kind of authentic joy. The Bible tells us things like, "Do not let the sun go down while you are still angry" (Ephesians 4:26 NIV), and "Confess your sins to each other and pray for each other so that you may be healed" (James 5:16 NIV). When we don't confess our sin to God and to each other, and when we let offenses linger, we leave room for laugh blockers to develop. We may have the joy, joy, joy, joy down in our hearts, but if our hearts are filled and clogged with offense, then that joy can't be released. So the key is to keep your heart free of offense so laughter can flow freely.

Danny: Amen! Preach it.

Where do you get all your costumes?

Danny: Since I can remember, there has always been a "prop box" in my life, filled with funny hats, wigs, and other random costuming items and props. It must have started while I was performing the variety shows with my family, and then my collection grew over time. I also loved "spirit week" at school, so needless to say, I always had something crazy to throw on. And then my wardrobe and prop collection grew even more once I moved out to Hollywood, as I routinely needed various wardrobes and props for miscellaneous auditions that would come up.

Kristin: Yeah, when we moved in together, seeing the plethora of boxes you owned with wigs and random items was definitely strange. I mean, if that's not a sign of a psychopath, I don't know what is.

Danny: Bwahahaha!

Kristin: At the same time, it wasn't completely out of the ordinary for me either. One of the networks I worked for back in my television hosting days had skits and sketches on their shows, so I would acquire various costumes from the wardrobe department over the years. And when the network folded, they had a wardrobe sale, so we stocked up big-time.

Danny: We got prison suits, mechanic outfits, and all kinds of shoes and costume jewelry, because, hey, you never know when you're going to need any of that. And then, another network (MadTV) ended as well, so we scored on even more authentic costuming at their wardrobe sale.

Kristin: Plus, you had your one-man comedy show where we acquired outfits for all your original characters, so by the time we left LA, our garage was full of wardrobe racks and a ridiculous amount of bins full of wigs and props. We essentially moved a mini–prop house across the country to Indiana.

Danny: And then, once we started doing the lip syncs where we changed fifteen to twenty times per video, impersonating specific music artists or characters from movies, our wardrobe no longer sufficed. So I researched costume shops in Indianapolis and discovered an amazing, authentic costume store called Costumes by Margie. This place was literally five thousand square feet of top-to-bottom theater-grade costumes. We were blown away to find a shop like this in Indianapolis. We established a rapport with the owner of the shop, and once she was fully on board to help us (for example, styling our outfits and wigs and loaning us the costumes at little to no charge) we were able to up the creativity of our lip sync videos.

Kristin: The shop owner, Cheryl, coming on board was a game changer. She helped take our lip syncs to another level.

Danny: Sadly, the COVID-19 pandemic put her store out of business, but we are forever grateful for all she did for us. I would often be at the shop until the wee hours of the morning, putting outfits together as Cheryl styled all the wigs. We all made some memories together for sure. If you like the costuming in our lip syncs like "The Greatest Showman," "Christmas Movies," "Love Songs of the Decades," and "80s Songs" or "80s Movies," then you have Cheryl to thank.

Kristin: Thank you, Cheryl!

Danny: When her shop closed this past summer, we purchased a ton of things during their liquidation sale. With all that we purchased, along with the things Cheryl gifted to us, we essentially doubled our inventory. So we did what any normal, suburban married couple would do and converted our basement storage closet into a mini costume store.

Kristin: Yep, we're officially the people with creepy mannequin heads and wigs hanging on their walls. Let's just say that I no longer go down to the basement alone.

Us and the kids dressed as The Flintstones while filming our "TV Show Theme Songs" lip sync video, 2017.

How long does it take to put together a lip sync video?

Danny: It typically takes us from one and a half to three weeks, depending on how creatively involved the costuming is and what we have going on in other areas of our life at that moment.

Kristin: The actual filming of each song or scene takes fifteen to thirty minutes, but when you add in the prep time of dressing up and getting into character, it's more like an hour for each one. If there are fifteen to twenty songs or scenes, then we have to shoot over the course of several days.

Danny: And since we film in the car, we deal with the sun moving and the light changing, so we have only a three- to four-hour window to film. Based on the intensity of the sunlight, and the angles at which it spills into the car, we often have to cover our car windows with blankets and towels, which only adds more time to filming each scene.

Kristin: And then you add in the preproduction time where we select the songs or scenes, decide which part of the song we are going to lip-sync or which part of the movie we are going to re-enact, download those clips and scenes and edit them into a rough timeline, and take multiple trips to the costume store.

Danny: And the postproduction time where I
    edit everything together and smooth out the
    sounds and transitions . . .

Kristin: Then you're looking at a couple of weeks
    when it's all said and done.

Danny: Here are the steps we took to create our
    most popular video to date, "Love Songs of
    the Decades":

- Make a list of our all-time favorite love songs. Creative brainstorming session on how we could bring a fun, unique, or comedic spin to our re-enactment of the song.
- Narrow down the list by picking our personal favorites, plus making sure we include diversity in the singers and genres while keeping the comedy aspect in mind.
- Go to the costume shop with our list and narrow it down to the final choices based on our costuming options.
- Take two or three evenings after-hours at the costume shop to pull clothes, finalize costumes, and style wigs.
- Bring home completed costumes and wigs. We typically set up a wardrobe rack in our bedroom and hang all the outfits in the order in which we plan to film. Since we do almost twenty songs each lip sync, this is roughly forty outfits!
- Film the video over the course of the next four to five days.

- Import the completed footage into our editing software as we go so Danny can start trimming and piecing things together, making sure we didn't forget anything.
- Return the outfits to the costume shop.
- Danny goes into the editing cave and edits for the next four to five days. Kristin slides his meals underneath the door.
- We check and double-check everything, then Kristin preps the social media posts, prepares a thumbnail, writes the copy, makes sure the video is tagged properly, and then publishes it on all of our social channels.

What's the coolest opportunity that has come out of making viral videos?

Kristin: Oh, that's a good one. We've had so many, but this book is definitely up there!

Danny: Yes, and traveling the county, being able to bring laughter and share our story and encourage other married couples along their journeys. Seeing a lot of small-town America has been enjoyable too, which we've highlighted in our online series, "Local Treasures." We were even given the key to Madison, Indiana.

Kristin: We're still trying to figure out which doors that key opens. One of the unique opportunities we've had was being in the

Indianapolis 500 Parade as a family, which was pretty awesome.

Danny: Yes! Especially since Indy is my hometown. When I was growing up, watching the parade was such a big deal. So to be invited to be in it was such an honor, it was so much fun to get into costume with the kids and ride through the streets of downtown.

Our family riding in the 2018 Indianapolis 500 Festival Parade, dressed in The Greatest Showman–themed attire.

Jeffrey Brown/Icon Sportswire via Getty Images

What do your neighbors think?

Kristin: Back when we were living and shooting videos in Los Angeles, seeing a neighbor shooting a video while dressed in costume wasn't necessarily odd. It's La La Land, right? It was more or less par for the course to see someone walking down the street in a costume there. That's just another typical day in LA.

Danny: However, once we moved back to the Midwest, where most people work more traditional nine-to-five jobs, seeing us sitting in our car wearing multiple costumes and wigs definitely raised some eyebrows! So when we moved to Indiana, one of the first things we did was make friends with our new neighbors. We broke the ice early on and explained to them "what we did for a living." Better that they hear it from us directly rather than seeing racks of costumes and wigs in our garage, with no context whatsoever. Hopefully we saved a lot of concerning conversations around their dinner tables.

Kristin: Gah, who are we kidding? They for sure still talked about us.

Danny: True. I mean, they regularly endured seeing me come out of the house in gym attire one day and man-sized dresses the next.

Kristin: Not to mention that when we shoot our lip sync vids, we typically film four to five outfits per day over the course of a few days. So they see each of us come in and out of the house in thirty minute increments . . .

Danny: never going anywhere . . . just in and out of the front seat of our car . . .

Kristin: wearing all kinds of craziness.

Danny: But seriously, once they started seeing our videos and how everything looks when it is all put together, they loved it. They not only share our videos but also help us out by lending all sorts of props that we need when we're filming.

Kristin: We'll always think of something last minute or get an impromptu idea where we need some type of food or instrument—

Danny: or walkie-talkies and a NERF gun we could use to be the Ghostbusters.

Kristin: The best is when we knock on their door, in full costume, asking for these things.

Danny: Like the time we knocked on the neighbor's door as John Lennon and Yoko Ono, asking to borrow an old-school corded telephone.

Kristin: Yes! Most neighbors just ask to borrow some milk or sugar. Not us.